young muslim voices

Volume 5

Writings by
Essay Panel Contest
Participants

Published by Mafiq Foundation
Silver Spring, Maryland

Copyright © 2012 by Mafiq Foundation, Inc.

All rights reserved. No part of this publication may be reproduced, stored in a retrieval system, transmitted or utilized, in any form or by any means, electronic, mechanical, photocopying, recording or otherwise, without the prior permission of the publisher.

ISBN-13: 978-0-9700372-1-3

Printed in the United States of America

Publisher
Mafiq Foundation, Inc.
P. O. Box 4916
Silver Spring, Maryland 20914-4916
U. S. A
Tel: (301) 236-0233
Website: http://epc.mafiq.org

Contents

Essay Panel Contest
January 14, 2012
Dar Al-Noor Islamic Community Center, Manassas, Va.

Graphic Dedication v
Dedication vii
EPC Steering and Editorial Committees viii
Foreword ix
Preface xi
A Reflection on the EPC Judging Process xiii

Introduction 1

Patience: What Does It Mean to Me?

Level 1 – Grades 1 & 2 7
Level 2 – Grades 3 & 4 15

Patience: How Do I Achieve It?

Level 3 – Grades 5 & 6 25
Level 4 – Grades 7 & 8 37

Patience and Perseverance in Times of Trials and Tribulations

Level 5 – Grades 9 & 10 49
Level 6 – Grades 11 through College 63

Appendix A: From the EPC Community 77

Appendix B: EPC Guidelines for 2011 79

Appendix C: Glossary of Arabic/Islamic Terms 83

Dedicated to those who patiently wait for rewards from Allah alone.

epc

young muslim voices: volume 5

"A beautiful patience [should be my course]; and Allah is the One to take refuge in from the things you assert." Surah Yusuf, 12:18

Design by Raadia Khan

This book is dedicated to all of the parents of past and future Essay Panel Contest participants who work to please Allah (swt) by following His Teachings and His Final Messenger (sas).

To mightier pens, sharper minds, and in pursuit of the most beautiful of patience.

"Only those who are patient shall receive their reward in full, without reckoning."
Al-Quran (Surah Az Zumar 39:10)

Narrated Abu Hurairah (ra) Allah's Messenger (sas) said, "The example of a believer is that of a fresh tender plant; from whatever direction the wind comes, it bends it, but when the wind becomes quiet, it becomes straight again. Similarly, a believer is afflicted with calamities (but he remains patient till Allah removes his difficulties.) And an impious wicked person is like a pine tree which keeps hard and straight till Allah cuts (breaks) it down when He wishes."
Al-Bukhari; Vol. 7, Book 70, Hadith #547

"O you who believe! Seek help with patience and prayer (as-salaat). Surely Allah is with those who are patient (as-sabirun)."
Al-Quran (Surah Al Baqarah, 2:153)

EPC Steering Committee:

Farid Ahmed, Ph.D.
Zahra Ahmed, M.D.
Mohammad S. Choudhury, Ph.D.
Mostafiz R. Chowdhury, Ph.D.
Susan Jenkins, Ph.D.
Kashif Munir, M.D.
Ayman Nassar, M.Sc.

Editorial Committee:

Fatimah Waseem, Editor-in-Chief
Farid Ahmed, Ph.D.
Zahra Ahmed, M.D.
Mohammad S. Choudhury, Ph.D.
Zahirah Eppard
Susan Jenkins, Ph.D.

Graphic Design: Sakina Productions

Foreword

"You're going to be a published author!" an organizer from the Mafiq Foundation happily told me. "From this year on, every winning entry will be published in a book by Mafiq Foundation Insha'Allah!"

Talk about an early Eid present. I found it difficult to believe that my thoughts were significant enough to be published in an actual, physical, bound book. At this time when I doubted even myself, unsure if I really had anything unique to offer to the world, the sincere team from Mafiq Foundation trusted in my work and that of my peers. Months later, I held a book in my hands with my own name and words imprinted upon its pages. It was an emotional moment.

Since then, this same moment has been experienced by many Muslim youth that have carried the torch and spirit of the Essay Panel Competition (EPC) forward. They wrote and spoke fervently, understanding that it was the due to the tireless efforts of the organizers, judges, and their parents, that they have been given a platform to write upon, a pulpit to speak upon, and a shoulder to lean upon. With that same passion and vigor, many of these youth are now contributing back to the fabric of American society with a unique and fresh perspective that stemmed from their experiences at this Muslim competition.

It is with competitions such as EPC that the youth are given a chance to voice their own thoughts and to have them heard with serious analysis and consideration from adult members of the community. When they stand on stage and accept an award for their winning papers and speeches, they are given recognition, a boost of self-esteem, and above all, acceptance. For the children that are used to being relegated to childcare at Muslim functions and are reprimanded for speaking back to their respected elders, it is with competitions such as EPC that they are finally brought to the spotlight and given a medium to share what they find important and hold close and dear to them.

Reflecting back, I realize it was the exposure to the Islamic literary world from EPC that inspired me to continue to read and write, and eventually found Muslim Youth Musings, an award-winning literary magazine that publishes quality literature by Muslim youth. I am frequently asked if the writing is mainly geared to the Muslim youth and much to their surprise, I tell them that it actually isn't, that the aspect of youth only comes from the writers themselves. From my experiences with EPC, I have come to understand that the youth have a story to tell not just to their peers, but to the entire world.

It is with these opening remarks that I introduce you to the fifth volume of *Young Muslim Voices*. I invite you to read these heartfelt essays on patience written by youth from the early years of first grade to the final years of high school. Above all, I ask that you pray for these young men and women, that their voices go heard, that their aspirations are met, and that their words go far.

Arif A. Kabir
Editor in Chief
Muslim Youth Musings

Preface

All praises be to Allah (swt) for the fifth volume of Essay Panel Contest (EPC) publications. Young Muslim brothers and sisters of Washington DC metro area wrote these essays based on the theme patience – "Verily the steadfast and those who patiently persevere will truly receive a reward without measure" (39:10).

A Muslim needs to achieve this great virtue (patience) as mentioned by Allah (swt) and exemplified by his prophets and messengers.

These writings are a reflection of the understanding and comprehension of patience by the contemporary Muslim youth. These young writers patiently worked on their essays and internalized this great virtue themselves in the process as well. InshaAllah, this publication will give our youth a sense of accomplishment, confidence, and encouragement to excel in their learning and writing skills.

Please spread the word. I encourage the Muslim youth to keep up their efforts in learning and writing.

Oh Allah, make us patient and follow the way of Muhammad (sas).
Oh Allah, give our youth knowledge and wisdom.
Oh Allah, accept our efforts. Ameen.

Mohammad O. Mahboob
President
Mafiq Foundation, Inc.

A Reflection on the EPC Judging Process

Al-sabr, often translated as 'patience' in English, has many places within our lives and deen. We too often equate it only with enduring hardships. Those with greater understanding add on thankfulness and gratitude while facing adversity. Patience of course has many deeper levels we sometimes neglect or forget: calmness and composure; controlling our anger; maintaining good character; grit and fortitude when trials become increasingly laborious; restraint; tolerance; maintaining focus and balance when others have given up, all the while remembering, thanking and praising the Almighty, Allah (swt).

Calamity or travail often leads to a feeling of solitude, grief and stress. These are the moments of life's tests. These are the moments weighed heaviest on the scales. These are the moments where patience is requisite.

Present day culture and society move rapidly and are getting increasingly faster. People no longer have time to eat, or sleep or maintain personal social relations without commotion. Screens occupy countless hours of our day, keeping us distracted from the relationships we must foster, the duties we must fulfill. Many who do take the time to remember their Creator do so in a rushed manner with minds racing, thoughts fleeting, hearts straying. Patience may be the one virtue we are currently more in need of than any other.

In this, the fifth volume of *Young Muslim Voices*, our youth explore the question of patience and how it impacts their lives. What does patience mean to them, how do they achieve it and what are the lessons we can learn from trials and tribulations. This publication arises from an annual essay competition we hold to encourage the youth to identify challenges which face them, critically analyze these challenges and develop viable solutions. Our goal is to help develop writers, orators, thinkers and leaders to command the next generation.

We are indebted to all of those individuals who have sacrificed their time and efforts in this collective good for our youth. The volunteers and judges for these competitions are to be commended for their true commitment and patience in this endeavor. May Allah bless their perseverance and strivings for His cause.

We appreciate your continued support for the annual essay and speech competition along with the yearly debate competition sponsored by the MAFIQ foundation. We feel both have become necessary forums for young Muslims to express their hopes and expectations for our future.

Kashif Munir, M.D.
Chair
Judges Panel

بِسْمِ اللهِ الرَّحْمٰنِ الرَّحِيْمِ

Introduction

This issue of the *Young Muslim Voices* (YMV), Volume 5 – written by students ranging from first grade to college – presents a snapshot of on patience by a diverse group of Muslim youth growing up in the Metropolitan Washington, D.C. area. The ideas expressed in this volume are reflections of the authors' mindset, environment, upbringing, and the values they have entertained. The youth have written simple, ordinary essays but the message embedded in the collection presented in this volume and those in the past four YMV volumes has extraordinary implications on the refreshing insights of their progression, capacity, and intellectual possibilities. We are indebted and grateful to Allah (swt) for allowing us to be a part of the annual Essay Panel Contest (EPC) platform that provides an opportunity to promote and encourage youth to practice and test their imagination and foster solid communication skills.

EPC has consistently served the community since 2002 and a number of our regular past youth participants have already established themselves as good role models for the community. Our Young Muslim Voices series reflects the impact and the possibility of this platform in boosting the morale of our youth and instilling in them a sense of accomplishment and confidence. Returning participants have demonstrated significant improvement year after year in their communication and leadership skills. The potential of EPC is immense and the extraordinary undertaking that has emerged is remarkable. New initiatives such as a research internship to engage our college-bound students in critical thinking and solving community issues using a scientific approach, and community service projects for the high school students are emerging out of this platform. The road leading to such innovative ideas is wide open. It is, however, the commitment, dedication, sincerity, and unwavering determination of the organizers and a constant reliance on Allah's (swt) mercy and forgiveness that are the source of our inspiration. The possibility of building an institution to help produce the next generation of thinkers and leaders could never be imagined without the hard work, determination, and steadfastness of our dedicated core groups, steering committee, organizational committee, volunteer judges, sponsors, and parents. They are the cornerstone of this success and without their joint and sustained effort and support we could not be here to see the wide horizon that is opening up to us.

Thus, EPC has grown beyond a mere Essay Panel Contest, as it was originally planned. It serves to:

- **Encourage** our youth to enhance their knowledge of the deen and the dunya;

- **Prepare** them for public speaking and dissemination of different modes of communication including essay, panel, debate, poster, and multimedia presentation by offering a number of workshops and training sessions; and

- **Coordinate** events to foster competitive engagement among our youth.

We hope to continue working towards achieving these noble goals, inshaAllah.

EPC Program Structure

A brief outline of the EPC format is provided below for those who are not familiar with the process or who might like to replicate the program in their community.

First, an overall theme is determined that relates to our everyday experiences as Muslims in this society. Essay contest topics are then selected to encourage youth to ponder difficult Islamic subjects while increasing their eman, and expanding their cognitive and analytical skills, insha Allah.

Each year, students from first grade to college compete in a theme-based essay contest. In the first round, the participants write an essay based on specific guidelines for submission. There are three development-based levels of competition: elementary school, middle school, and high school/college. The goal for the elementary category is to epitomize the foundation and principles of Islam and its message. The middle school category essay topics focus on matters concerning character building and morality; and the high school topics require reflection on and analysis of contemporary issues. The first-round essays are scored and ranked; the authors of the top-ranked essays then participate in a second-round speech competition. Eventually, a collection of the best essays is compiled and published in our Young Muslim Voices series. Moreover, EPC extends beyond the written and spoken word to include poster and multimedia competitions. These two creative components of the contest, like their counterparts, have had resounding success as they are continually expanding in new directions.

Introduction 3

The central theme of the EPC for the year 2011 was "Patience." Participants were asked to:

- **Expound** on what patience means to them, what role it plays in their life, and how and why they treasure it (in Levels 1 and 2);

- **Reflect** on how patience can be achieved, specifically by drawing from historical examples and inspirational figures (in Levels 3 and 4); and

- **Analyze** how to best exercise patience in light of trials and tribulations (in Levels 5 and 6).

We hope that you enjoy reading the essays as much as we did, and are amazed by the participants' ability to analyze complex issues and settle them in an amicable way.

We Need Your Help

The efforts to organize and implement the Essay Panel Contests each year require a significant amount of time, manpower, and money. To date, the competitions were sponsored by generous contributors and were organized and implemented solely by volunteers. As we look toward future expansion, we will need more sponsors and more hands to accomplish this task.

We invite you become a part of these efforts – with your own ideas, energy or financial contributions, Please contact Br. Mostafiz Chowdhury at essays@Mafiq.org. And by all means, please keep us in your dua'as.

EPC Steering Committee

Disclaimer: YMV publications and EPC activities of Mafiq Foundation, Inc. are solely for informative and educational purposes. The opinions and views expressed by the authors and presenters are their sole and separate views and opinions and do not necessarily reflect those of the EPC steering Committee, nor does the Mafiq Foundation adopt such opinions or views as its own.

Essay Panel Contest
2011

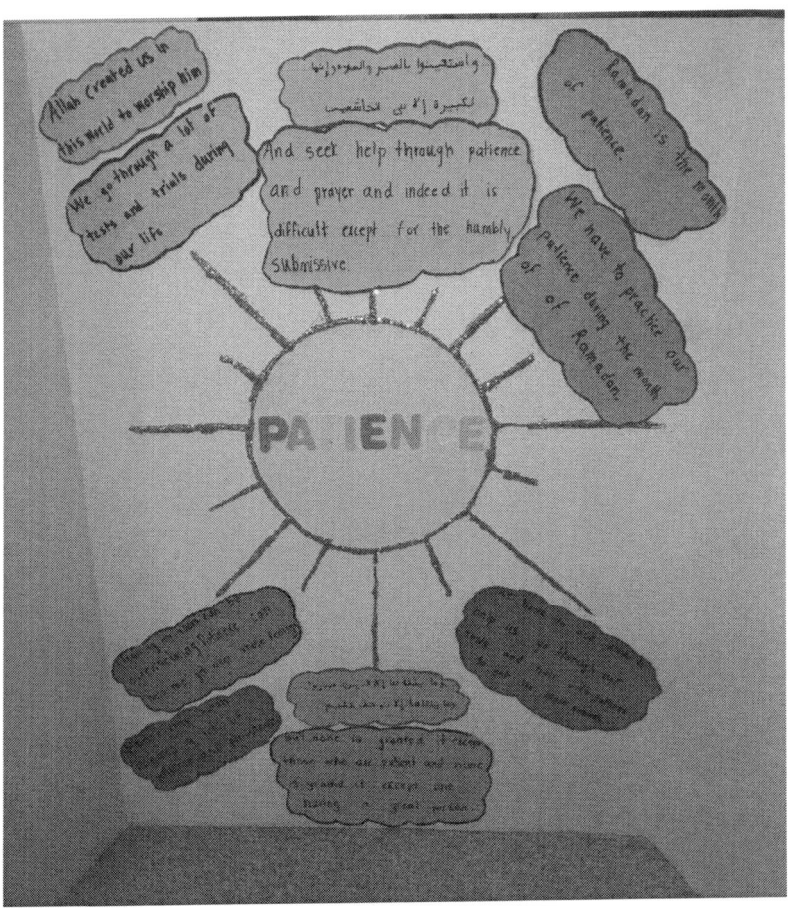

This poster was submitted by Hadeel Abdulmageed and won 1st Place honors in Level 2.

*Patience:
What Does It Mean to Me?*

LEVEL 1: Grades 1 & 2

1st Place
Noorah Ahmed, College Park, Md.
2nd Grade, Homeschool

Dear Zeenat,

Assalaamu Alaikum. I am writing this letter to you to tell you about patience in Islam. Remember that time you became angry with your little cousin? Well, that wasn't called being patient. I have learned a little about patience and I want to tell you about it. Patience means to wait and to be calm. When you are patient, Allah (swt) is happy with you. Allah loves people who are patient. My mom and dad say that if we are patient here on Earth, Allah will reward us with all the good things in Jannah inshaAllah. And Allah (swt) tells us in the Quran that, "Only those who are patient shall receive their reward in full without reckoning" (Surah 39:10).

There are many times when I have to try to be patient. It usually happens at home when my little sister and I are playing. Sometimes when she wants to play a game that I don't want to, I either make a deal with her to play my game too or I will just play her game. This is one way I show patience. Another way is when my little brother Saadiq wants one of my toys. I don't mind sharing, but he breaks my toys sometimes. But my mom reminds me that we can always get a new toy. So then I am patient and let him play with them, even if he breaks them. I also try to be patient when my parents tell me that they can't read a book to me sometimes. I wait calmly and then my older sister will read the book to me. If I don't get upset, Allah (swt) helps me get what I want, alhamdulillah. So you see Zeenat, it is great to have patience. Many good things happen when we are patient. And remember Allah loves those who are patient. Write back soon. Assalaamu Alaikum.

> Love,
> Noorah

2nd Place
Musa Ahmad, Greenbelt, Md.
2nd Grade, Tarbiyyah Academy

Dear Mastathi,

Assalaamu alaikum, How are you and your family? I am writing this letter to you because I need to write an essay to someone about patience. You need a lot of patience because you have a lot of kids. Allah (swt) says in the Quran: "O you who believe, seek help in patience and prayer, Allah is with those who are patient" (2:153). So Allah (swt) will be with you if you are patient.

If you are somewhere and all your kids are running around and shouting, you might get annoyed, but you need to have a lot of patience. You should not shout at them. You should call them to you nicely. If my sister takes my favorite toy, I have to be patient and ask her if I could have my toy. If she says no, then I have to ask my parents to tell her to give it back and not get upset.

If you are ready to go somewhere and one of your kids gets out of the car and they go inside and for a long time they don't come out, you need to wait for them patiently. If you are not patient, then Allah (swt) will not be with you.

When I am in the car and I get hungry, I always try to be patient because some poor people do not even have anything to eat or drink. If I don't have patience, then I am ungrateful to Allah (swt), for what I have.

I hope you and your family enjoyed reading this letter.

With love from your nephew,
Musa

3rd Place
Hareez Saiyed, Woodbridge, Va.
2nd Grade, Antietam Elementary School

Assalaamu Alaikum. I would like to talk about patience with you because I saw you were not patient with your younger brother and sister.

Allah (swt) says being patient is very, very important. There are many suraat, like Al-Baqarah Al-A'raaf, Yusuf, Ibrahim, Al-Nahl, Al-Kahaf, Al- Mu'minoon. Al-Ahqaf, Al-Tur, Al-Qamar, and Al-Ma'arij where He tells us about patience. So that's why you have to be patient and if you are not patient you might go to the hellfire. And if you are patient you might go to Jannah. So be careful and be patient. Did you know that Prophet Muhammad (sas) practiced patience and that's how he made lots of people join him and that's the second reason why you have to be patient. And, note that Prophet Muhammad (sas) not only practiced, he was also very patient man.

My aunt is very patient, my brothers and sisters are patient, but my baby sister is not that patient. I am sometimes patient, my mom and dad are patient, my uncle is very patient, my grandma is also very patient. Technically my whole family is patient. I am patient when I am in the car and we still have a long way to go. I am not patient when a family member of mine is talking when I am talking.

So, in summary, I talked about why you should be very, very patient and the suraat that have the word patience in them and about how Muhammad (sas) was patient. I hope you will start being patient with your family.

Love,
Hareez

Special Essay
Samihah Farooqi, Springfield, Va.
4th Grade*, Iqra Academy

Dear Navairah,

Assalaamu Alaikum! I am going to tell you about patience. Patience means bearing of provocation, arrogance, misfortune, or pain without complaint, loss of temper, or anger. Patience means to me that if I get in trouble or have a hard time, I should not get upset or angry. Instead I should be patient and ask help from Allah (swt). Try to be patient and ask help from Allah (swt). Try to be patient all the time. Do not get angry or annoyed. If I am being patient all the time I can get plenty of rewards from Allah (swt).

If someone tries to argue with me I should be patient. If my little brother messes up my homework or an important paper I should not get angry. If I am traveling and if we are stuck in traffic I should try to be patient and not bother my mom or dad by asking questions like, "Are we there yet?"

I show patience when I get hurt by not crying or getting upset. I show patience when my parents ask me to do something while I am watching my favorite TV show. I turn off the TV and do what my parents told me. I show patience when my little brother tries to snatch things away from me. I do not fight back with him and remain gentle with him and I show sabr.

I try to encourage myself to be patient with my siblings, cousins, and friends. I encourage my sister to be patient with me, our cousins and our friends. I try to encourage my cousins to be patient a lot because they fight so much. Prophet Nuh (as) was patient when he taught Islam for 950 years and only 72 people accepted Islam. Prophet Ismail (as) showed sabr when his dad, Prophet Ibrahim (as), had a command that he had to slaughter his son and replied, "Okay father, do as you are told." Prophet Ayub (as) showed lots of patience in his life because he got severely sick and all his wealth and family and whatever he owned was gone. It was a big test from Allah (swt) but he didn't say a word. He showed a great deal of patience for all of us to learn from.

Sabr is the most important part of our faith. Allah (swt) will be very happy for the person who is patient. Allah (swt) said, "Seek help with patience and As-Salat (the prayer)." The Messenger of Allah (sas) said: "How wonderful is the case of a believer. There is good for him in everything and this applied only to a believer. If prosperity attends him, he expresses gratitude to Allah (swt) and that is good for him and if adversity befalls him, he endures it patiently and that is better for him." In order to get awards from Allah (swt), we should be patient.

Sincerely,
Your sister in Islam

*A registration oversight; participant mistakenly submitted her essay in this level.

Special Speech
Jannah Nassar, Clarksville, Md.
2nd Grade, Clarksville Elementary School

Assalaamu Alaikum Maryum,

I will talk about how I am patient every day. When I wake up, I ask mama if my lunch is ready. If she says no, I go and get my snack and juice ready. I get my lunch and go to the bus. I am patient at the bus stop and I am not asking when the bus is coming. At school, I am patient by going to my class. I put my stuff away quietly instead of talking and being loud. I choose to be patient because Prophet Muhammad (sas) was patient. My sister told me that Allah (swt) protects people who are patient. Allah (swt) loves people who are patient. In Surah Al 'Imran, Allah (swt) loves those who are patient. I try to be patient because I want Allah (swt) to love me.

I know a story about a prophet who was not patient. His name was Prophet Yunus (as). Prophet Yunus (as) stopped being patient when his people would not listen to the message of Islam. Allah (swt) tested him and took away his support and made him get thrown in the ocean. In the ocean, he was swallowed by a whale. When he was in the whale's stomach, he realized that he was not patient and then he asked Allah (swt) to forgive him and Allah (swt) forgave him.

I am patient at home, at school, and with my sisters even if they annoy me. It is hard to be patient. You should be patient no matter where you are because you should always obey Allah (swt). Sometimes it is hard for me to be patient but I try to be patient and so should you.

Love,
Jannah

Essay Panel Contest
2011

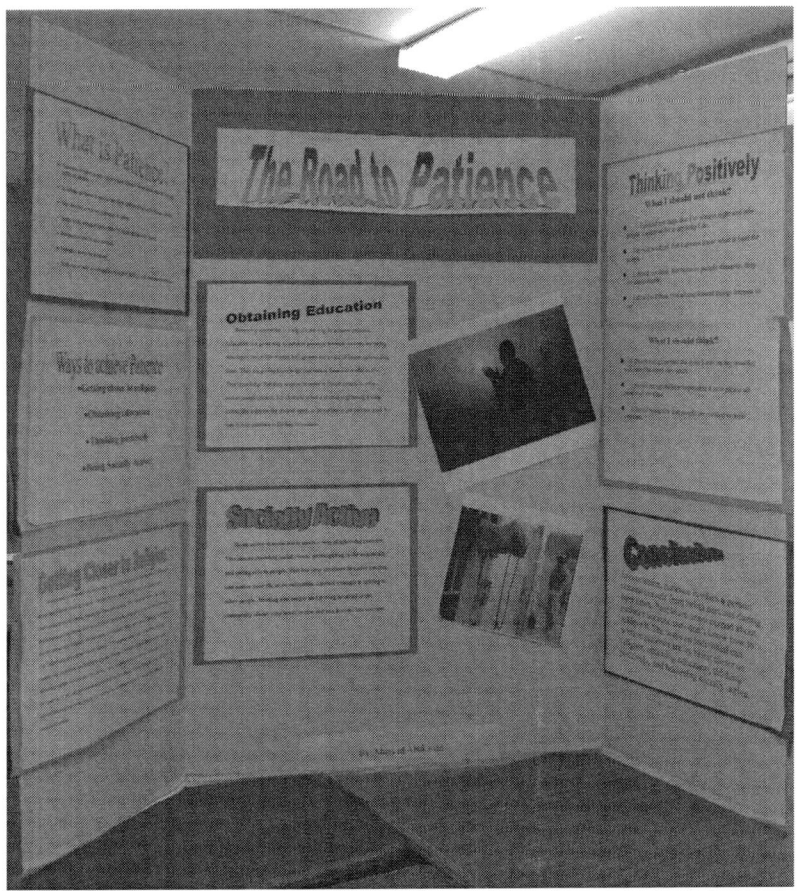

This poster was submitted by Muayad Abukanan and won 1st Place honors in Level 3.

Patience: What Does It Mean to Me?

LEVEL 2: Grades 3 & 4

1st Place
Noor Mansoor, Woodbridge, Va.
3rd Grade, Prince William Academy

Dear little sister and brother,

I am writing a letter to encourage you both to be patient and grateful to Allah (swt) for all that we have alhamdulillah. Patience is waiting without fussing or getting upset. For example, I try to be patient by waiting my turn and not interrupting when someone else is talking, even if I have to say something very important. When we are stuck in traffic, we should not keep asking our parents, "When will we get there?" We should try to sit patiently and wait until we get to where we are going. The Quran says, "Be patient for your patience is with the help of Allah (swt)" (16:127). There are so many people who have much less than we do, but they are patient and thankful to Allah (swt).

Did mommy ever tell you both the story about our grandparents? Well, they both went through very hard times. Our grandfather's family used to live in India during the time there was a war going on. They had to flee to Pakistan. Our grandfather's dad, uncle, and grandfather died before they could make it to Pakistan. Our grandfather and his many siblings grew up without a father. Dealing with the sadness of the passing away of a loved one also requires patience. Our grandmother went through many hardships as well. She grew up without a father too. We think our hardships are big deals but they are nothing compared to our grandparents' hard times.

The Prophet (sas) and his companions (ra) went through even more difficult times and were tested. Prophet Ayub (as)'s crops died, then his kids died, and he became very ill; yet he did not complain. The nonbelievers would place heavy stones on Bilal (ra)'s chest, but he would still say Ahad, meaning "the one Allah." They would throw stones at Prophet Muhammad (sas) and still he was patient and did not give up telling them about Islam. We should try to be more patient everyday so Allah (swt) is pleased with us.

A good time to learn about patience is during Ramadan. In Ramadan, we control our hunger and anger. We should try to stay calm and not fight with each other. It comes in a hadith that, "Calmness and patient deliberation is from Allah (swt) and haste is from shaytan" (Tirmidhi).

I try to practice being patient in my everyday life. We should accompany our parents to the shelter so we can help people who have less than us. It will also make us more thankful to Allah (swt) for everything we have. There are people all over the world who do not even have a shelter, food, water and clothes. Allah (swt) has given us a lot, but He can take it all away too if He wants. Whatever the case is we should always remain patient. There is a beautiful Quran ayah that says, "And certainly, We shall test you with something of fear, hunger, loss of wealth, lives and fruits, but give glad tidings to As-Sabirun (the patient)" (2:155).

May Allah (swt) make us good and righteous children and help us practice patience in our everyday life. Ameen.

Love,
Your big sis.

2nd Place
Nowshin Shaira, Centreville, Va.
3rd Grade, London Towne Elementary School

You walk into the cafeteria, your stomach growling with hunger. The cafeteria line is huge, from one side of the cafeteria to the other. "Oh no, how can I wait that long," you think to yourself.

"Just have patience," a random person says.

Patience is a great quality of life. It means putting up with pains or hardships calmly or without complaint and showing self-control. Without it, you can't wait for anything to be over. Without it, if you don't like reading, you wouldn't want to read this essay. Here, I will explain what it means to be patient and how I show it in my daily life.

Patience is a person's ability to control anger, emotion, and troubling situations. When you are patient, you calmly wait for something, you are at a peace of mind, and you are cool and calm about the future. If not, you have trouble that brings you worry and stress.

"And certainly, we shall test you with something of fear, hunger, loss of wealth, lives and fruits, but give glad tidings to As-Sabirun (the patient)" (2:155).

Sometimes people don't have patience in their self, like: listening, following instructions, and waiting for someone to finish talking. An example of patience is if a friend accidently messes up your artwork. Do not be angry. Everybody makes mistakes. In Islamic history, Prophet Muhammad (sas) shows us perfect examples of being patient. When he was faced with the harassment of Abu Lahab and the people of Ta'if, he never lost patience with them and still tried to preach to them.

Now I will give examples on how I show patience in my everyday life:

- Patiently waiting for my mom to finish prayer, then I can talk to my mother.
- Not rushing and taking my time on homework
- Raising my hand before I speak to my teacher
- Practice accepting, like if I want to buy a toy, but my parent says, "Not today."
- Waiting for my turn on the swings, in the cafeteria line, or my brother to finish his turn on his game before mine.
- Waiting for my teacher to finish the story book before asking questions.
- Waiting to open my Eid present until everyone is ready.

Abu Hurairah (ra) reported: The Messenger of Allah (sas) said, "Allah, the Exalted, says: 'I have no reward other than Jannah for a believing slave of Mine who remains patient for My sake when I take away his beloved one from among the inhabitants of the world'" (Al-Bukhari).

Patience is a very good quality to have. With it, we are cool and calm about the future. I use this quality by not rushing and practice accepting when things go wrong. Allah (swt) is very pleased with the patient. In fact, one of Allah's (swt) names is As-Saboor which means "The Patient." When you are patient you get blessings and guidance from Allah (swt), the ultimate reward.

Works Cited
Pettinger, Tejvan. "Benefits of Patience." Web. http://ezinearticles.com/?Benefits-of-Patience&id=496228

"Patience and Tips on How to Develop It." Essential Life Skills. Web. http://www.essentiallifeskills.net/patience.html

3rd Place
Abdullah Qidwai, Sterling, Va.
3rd Grade, Homeschool

Patience means many things. For example, it means not to hasten, but to take one's time doing whatever one's doing. It also means showing strength in the face of difficulty. That is, one waits calmly for one's wound to heal or for the problem to go away.

Patience can be learned from anyone, even children. As Franklin P. Jones, a Philadelphia reporter and humorist, once said, "You can learn many things from children. How much patience you have, for instance." Therefore, let me now give you some examples of my own to clarify what I understand about patience. It may be that both you and I will learn from these.

Whenever I build Legos with my younger brothers, they take too much time building their parts, but I have to be patient or else my mother would take the Legos away because we would start fighting. Also, when I get books from the library I try reading them all at once, but my mother advises me to be patient and read one book a day so that I could enjoy reading over time. Lastly, and more importantly, when I become impatient I get cranky and this in turn makes the whole family crabby, spoiling the day.

Patience is an important concept for Muslims. When a Muslim is in trouble, he or she must seek or ask for help from Allah (swt), both by being patient and by praying. This is exactly how it is mentioned in the Quran: "O you who believe! Seek help in patience and As-Salat (the prayer). Truly, Allah is with As-Sabirun (the patient)" (2:153).

It appears that Allah (swt) has given us a natural ability to be patient. Take the example of my youngest brother, Zayd. When he was learning how to climb the stairs a couple of years ago, he kept falling. Despite the continuous falls, he would keep trying until he finally mastered it. A Muslim can increase this natural ability to be patient by fasting in the month of Ramadan. Of course, how can one not learn to be patient when one does not eat or drink throughout the day, for 29 or 30 days continuously every year!

One could ask why Allah (swt) wants us to build patience in ourselves. I have already given the answer above when I described some of the meanings of the word patience. Allah (swt) wants us to have the calmness and strength that gives us the ability to practice His religion easily and to worship Him better and, therefore, become one of the righteous. Then, there is the reward too. Allah (swt) says, "Those [the righteous] will be rewarded with the highest place (in paradise) because of their patience. Therein, they shall be met with greetings and the word of peace and respect" (25:75).

Now, who would not want such a reward and not become patient?

Special Essay
Ameen Ahmed, College Park, Md.
3rd Grade, Hollywood Elementary

Sabr is an important quality that a Muslim should have. Sabr means to have patience. Patience means to be calm and do things without getting angry or frustrated. It means to be hopeful, too. When you're hopeful, you believe that something good will happen if you're patient. When you're patient it also means that you trust in Allah (swt). You believe that Allah (swt) knows everything and He has the best plans for you. In Surah Baqarah, ayah 153, Allah says, "Surely Allah is with the patient." He also says in Surah Al-Imran, ayah 146, "Allah loves those who are patient." SubhanAllah, if Allah (swt) is with those that are patient no matter what happens to them, then patience must be an important characteristic in Islam.

I don't always have patience. But as an older brother, my mom reminds me to be patient if my younger siblings are bothering me. It is very hard when they take my stuff. When I lose my patience my mom tells me to make du'a. By making dua'a, I'm focusing on asking Allah to help me. Allah says in Surah Baqarah, ayah 153 to "Seek help in patience and As-Salat." Another thing I do is take a deep breath and walk away. This is the hardest to do, but when I do it, it works, Alhamdulillah. I also have to be patient with my friends. I had to explain to them that I'm a Muslim, and that I shouldn't use bad words, or misbehave. When they tell me to do something I shouldn't do, I make dua'a to Allah (swt) to help them. This is another way to practice patience.

So, to me patience means to be calm no matter what. The Prophet (sas) was patient during many hardships he went through. If we just think about how the greatest man used to practice patience, it should make us do the same too. Insha Allah, let's all be more patient with one another and when things get tough.

Special Speech
Dleela Saiyed, Woodbridge, Va.
4th Grade, Antietam Elementary School

This essay is about patience. Patience is always important to have. If you didn't have patience, you couldn't do things like letting your little brother or sister watch TV during your favorite show. If you take the remote and put your show on, your brother or sister would tell on you. You would get in trouble for that. If you were patient, you wouldn't be in trouble.

Now we will talk more about patience. Prophet Muhammad (sas) was always patient. For example, when people didn't listen to Prophet Muhammad (sas), he was patient. When you are patient, people like you. Muhammad (sas) was always kind and patient. That is why he made so many people Muslims. People want what they like. Patient people get through things really well. There are many suraat that have patience mentioned in them. Nearly all the suraat that mention patience were revealed in Makkah which is important to know because during Makkan times, Muslims were given a very hard time.

When I am patient, I get good deeds. My dad is always patient when I ask him tons of questions.

I talked about patience and how people with patience are. You must be patient because it helps you at all times. When you are angry, you have to become very calm and patient. If you never have patience, how will you make friends? Sometimes your family gets very angry with you for not being patient. So remember this: if you never have patience you will never get through things. But if you do have patience you will get through things really well.

There are multiple ways I exercise patience in my house. For example, whenever I go to Taekwondo, my master always pushes me. But I am always patient and never give up. Whenever I go swimming, I get tired but I am always patient. When I get angry with my brothers and sisters for calling me names, I keep quiet and remain patient. I am always patient with my family. I stay in power with patience. When I am patient, I am working hard. I never give up. When I get angry, I try to be calm and patient. Patience is the thing that calms me down. I don't give up on things. I never yell or throw things at anybody. If my little brother watches TV and I want to watch also I have to be patient. I love having patience and what I do with it is just great. Patience is what makes everybody nice, calm, sweet, and other things as well. Patience is what makes people much nicer to other people. If somebody doesn't have patience, you could help him or her out and teach him or her how to control himself or herself. You could even help a family member. Sometimes families don't have patience at all. So just help people that don't have patience. People should always use patience whenever they can. That is what patience means to me.

Essay Panel Contest
2011

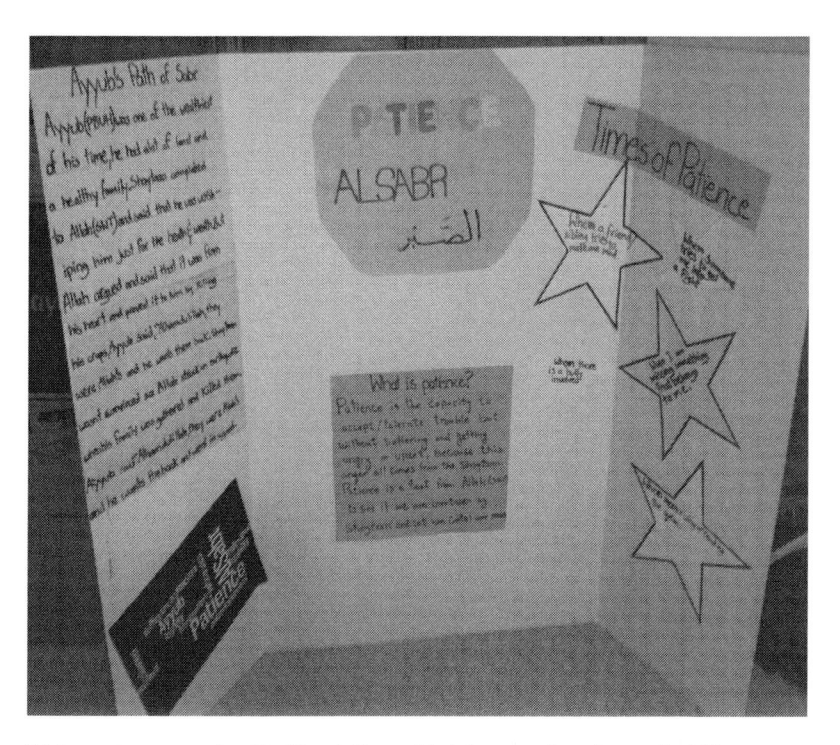

This poster was submitted by Adham Abdulmageed and won 2nd Place honors in Level 3.

Patience: How Do I Achieve It?

LEVEL 3: Grades 5 & 6

1st Place
Arsalan Ahmed Siddiqui, Beltsville, Md.
6th Grade, Dar-Us-Salam Hifz School

In Urdu, it is "sabar ka phal meetha hota hai." In Arabic, "Sabrun Jameelun." All mean the same thing: the fruit of patience is sweet. I heard this many times over and over again but I never understood its meaning until recently. It was talking about patience. In Islam, patience is one of the best and most valuable virtues for a prosperous life. In the Quran, Allah (swt) mentions patience a number of times. For example, he says, "Seek Allah's help with patient ...and prayer" (2: 45) and "Be steadfast in patience" (11:115). Prophets like Prophet Ayyub (as) and Prophet Yusuf (as) had enormous amounts of patience and from their trials, we can learn how to be patient as well.

Prophet Ayyub (as) had many animals, children and a large amount of wealth. He was also a healthy man. When his wealth, health, children, and animals were taken away from him, he was very patient. During his hardship, Prophet Ayyub (as) made remembrance of Allah (swt) – dhikr - and he never questioned the will of Allah (swt). I learned that you should have patience in whatever problems that you face. Have faith in Allah (swt) and never ask why this hardship is happening to me, just like Prophet Ayyub (as). For instance, everyday, I get loads of homework and I stay up finishing the work until 3 a.m. in the morning. I should not complain. Instead, I should do dhikr by thanking Allah (swt) that, alhamdulillah, He gave me an opportunity to memorize His glorious book, the Quran, and do homeschooling at the same time. This is how I can achieve patience, insha Allah.

Another example of being patient I take is from Prophet Yusuf's (as) life. When Prophet Yusuf's (as) brothers threw him in the well, Prophet Yusuf (as) did not take revenge on his brothers. Instead, he prayed to Allah (swt) and asked to give him patience and courage. Allah (swt) answered his dua'as by making his future very fortunate. Later, Yusuf (as) held a very high position as he became the chief minister of Egypt. I learned that you should be steadfast and patient by not panicking and making dhikr. Like Prophet Yusuf (as), forgive and forget other's mistakes. For example, I panic when I have a quiz. However, now I will remember the story of Prophet Yusuf (as); when he was thrown in the well and his life was in danger, he did not panic. My stress over the quiz is nothing compared to Prophet Yusuf's (as) trial but I can still take lessons from him. I should do dhikr and make dua'a for my quiz to be easy by placing my trust in the All-Mighty One. I will do better on the assessment with the help and mercy of Allah (swt).

Patience is when a person in times of hardship makes dhikr and has trust in Allah (swt). Soon, Allah (swt) will decrease his or her problems and he or she will have a prosperous future. From Islamic history, I learn that Prophet Ayyub (as) had patience and increased his good actions; soon Allah (swt) answered his dua'as and decreased his problems. Also, Prophet Yusuf (as) was patient through every obstacle he faced. When he was thrown in the well, he patiently waited for Allah's (swt) mercy and help. May Allah (swt) make us all like prophets who constantly made dhikr especially in times of hardship. Ameen ya rabb al-'alameen!

2nd Place
Sayeemah S. Ahmed, College Park, Md.
5th Grade, Al-Huda School

Have you ever wondered how to achieve sabr? Or have you even known what sabr meant? True, sabr means patience, but have you thought that it is much more than patience? Well, let's first look at this ayah, "And how many a prophet has had to fight [in God's cause], followed by many God-devoted men: and they did not become faint of heart for all that they had to suffer in God's cause, and neither did they weaken, nor did they abase themselves [before the enemy], since God loves those who are patient in adversity" (3:146). Reflecting on this ayah means to me that the prophets of Allah (swt) went through many hardships and pains. They never gave up and they never lost faith in Allah (swt). This is the way I should react to certain pains; I should remember that Allah (swt) is always on my side.

Sabr means patience, but it is more than patience. It means determination, courage, and perseverance. Sabr means to conquer your fear and to do the right thing even if you are in doubt. So why would this be beneficial to me? Well, if I ever get angry, I shouldn't let the anger conquer me, instead I should have the patience and cool down. It is beneficial, because that way I could be a stronger Muslim. As Prophet Muhammad (saw) said, "A strong person is not the person who throws his adversaries to the ground. A strong person is the person who contains himself when he is angry."

Sabr also helps me not to give up. Giving up is like losing faith in Allah (swt). Allah (swt) will always be around, why should I lose my faith? If I get a bad grade, I should not just stare at it; I should try to study harder for the next one. If sometimes my friends are being mean, I should just get along, and have patience. This is very beneficial, because my friend would learn a lesson that way, and at the same time, I will get the good deeds.

There is another great example in my life of how sabr helped me. I had to memorize a three-page surah for a Quran competition. It took all my patience to memorize the words of Allah (swt). I took it just step by step, which took a lot of perseverance. I went through the first step, the semifinal step, and alhamdulillah I was in the final round.

Even writing this essay was a great example of why being patient is beneficial. In the beginning, I was scared that I had to write 750 words on a topic like Sabr! I didn't think I could write that. But once I started and got determined, alhamdulillah I have almost written it. That's a great benefit of sabr.

So far, I have told you why sabr is beneficial in my life – to be a good Muslim, to be a good student, to be a good friend, to write this essay, and going to the final round of Quran competition. Now, I'll tell you what it takes to achieve this great virtue.

First I must tell you that going to Karate helped me have patience. The seven tenets of Karate are integrity, concentration, perseverance, respect and obedience, self-control, humility, and indomitable spirit. You can see that almost all these virtues lead to one simple thing – patience.

I can learn sabr from the Quran and hadith. As an example, Surah Asr taught me that being patient is one of the things that makes me not a loser. I think I should be patient, so I don't have to be a loser. Being a loser in that situation means I am being a loser to Allah (swt).

Another good way of practicing sabr is that I should decrease my whining and know what my real goal is. If I just say that being a Muslim is hard, I won't accomplish my real goal. Allah (swt) is very patient with us. I know I cannot be as patient as Allah (swt), but I should try to do my best and achieve this great virtue of being patient.

None of these will work if I don't have the help from Allah (swt). Let me then pray to Allah (swt) to give me patience, courage, determination, and perseverance. I will insha'Allah do my best and try to be patient so that Allah (swt) loves me, as He promised in Surah Al-Imran verse 146. Assalaamu Alaikum!

3rd Place
Huma Chowdhury, Laurel, Md.
6th Grade, Al-Huda School

"Patience serves as a protection against wrongs as clothes do against cold. For if you put on more clothes as the cold increases, it will have no power to hurt you. So, in like manner,, you must grow in patience when you meet with great wrongs, and they will then be powerless to vex your mind." This astounding quote from Leonardo Da Vinci tells the benefit of patience and its meaning. It isn't the meaning that we don't know; we do practice patience. At school, for example: waiting in line to get lunch; at home: giving siblings a turn to play game. How to achieve and practice patience is difficult. This is due to forgetfulness. I will explain how to achieve patience and how it's beneficial for us to succeed.

Allah (swt) tells us in Surah Al-Imran, ayah 146: "And many a prophet fought in Allah's cause and along with them fought large bands of religious learned men. But they never lost heart for that which did befall them in Allah's way, nor did they weaken nor degrade themselves. And Allah (swt) loves as Sabireen." This ayah says that all prophets and righteous people did have trials, and through patience they succeeded, so in order to succeed we will be tested. To pass these tests we must persevere. Allah (swt) is testing our level of Iman. Like prophet Nuh was tested for his patience with the people giving dawah for 950 years, prophet Ibrahim was tested to strengthen his belief and he was thrown in fire and he never gave up, Prophet Muhammad (sas) was tested for 13 years with terrible calamitous suffering to become the leader of mankind. The test and hardship is essential for success which is beneficial.

The ayah also says not to lose heart, meaning that they never lost their faith in Allah (swt). Also the ayah says to never weaken their hope and belief in Allah (swt) nor did they let themselves degrade; they never let themselves become like those who do nothing out of laziness. In relationship with Prophet Ibrahim (as), he was thrown into the blazing flames of hot fire. He never lost hope in that Allah (swt) would protect him. He also was courageous in not believing in idolism. Instead, he tried extremely hard to give da'wah to his people. And as you might have noticed, once the people have worked for their goal through patience, Allah (swt) does surely love them and He blesses them with great rewards here in this life and in the hereafter!

We need to know how to get that love from Allah (swt). To get that love we need patience. And to get patience we must practice step by step. It needs practice and time. Can we learn Chinese in one day? No. To achieve patience step by step, we must never lose our focus. Our focus is to become a righteous Muslim so we can enter Jannah. One level of patience is to suppress one's anger on others, like when one's irksome siblings might tear their homework, they keep anger in from letting it out on them. Likewise when practicing to become a swimmer or a hafiz, we must keep persevering. Now that one's got the hang of practicing patience, the next time Allah (swt) places us in a trial, we'll be ready because patience comes right back at us when we need it most, which is a great benefit. It's easy for a person to say salaam who practices every day, but it's hard for one who never practiced. When we don't lose our heart once hardships come upon us and don't give up nor degrade ourselves - then, we have achieved patience.

Hardship, pain, and suffering go for everyone who wants to succeed. Olympians like Apolo Ohno, for example, worked so hard day and night to get the gold medal; he never gave up. Ohno tried and went through a lot of pain to win the first prize for America. Even an elephant named Horton had patience while protecting a small world on a speck of dust from the evil people around him trying to destroy it; it kept on persevering to keep the small world together. After the suffering, he succeeded in keeping the small world alive.

Whether it is a prophet preaching his people for years without much result, an elephant patiently protecting a small world on a speck of dust, or an Olympian working hard to get the golden trophy, in all cases, sabr does win the race. We may forget to practice patience so we must turn to Allah (swt) for help and not to forget to be patient. And to reach your goal you must never lose heart, never weaken nor degrade yourself. Therefore, it sets things straight for you and it will never leave you stranded when you will most need it. Because once you've got the hang of practicing patience it becomes your personality. So I strongly deem that patience is the ultimate protection to never let the wrong acts or decisions befuddle your mind!

Special Essay
Layla Gholston, Columbia, Md.
6th Grade, Homeschool

There is an old African tale about a young married couple. The husband was not happy, so he began to come in late from the fields. His behavior made the wife miserable. One day, she went to the village elder to ask for help. The elder knew of a potion that would make her husband loving, but he was missing a special ingredient, and was too old to get it: the single whisker from a living lion. The wife agreed to get it. The next morning, she carried raw meat to where the lions might roam. After many hours, a lion came and ate it quickly and left. The next day, and the next and for many more weeks, the wife came back to try to get the whisker. Finally, one day, she pulled the whisker from the lion's chin and hurried off. The elder was in awe when he heard her story and told her she didn't need a potion to change her husband. If she could take a lion's whisker, she could have enough patience with her husband too. So she took the elder's advice, and slowly, her husband returned to his loving self.

This tale shows that patience could not only give a husband time to become loving, but patience can change a life. As Allah (swt) says in the Quran, "Patience is beautiful" and "Allah surely loves those who are the Sabireen." From these two statements in the Quran, I know that having sabr will bring me closer to Allah (swt). Being closer to Allah (swt) through patience will help me face the tests that come my way in a positive manner, and I will seek out patience by being a more reflective person.

Being impatient in the face of danger could cause someone to be irrational and get hurt. As the Chinese proverb says, "A moment of patience can prevent a great disaster and a moment of impatience can ruin a whole life." In Surah Al-Imran, ayah 146, Allah (swt) says, "And many a Prophet fought and along with him large bands of religious learned men. But they never lost heart for that which did befall them in Allah's Way, nor did they weaken nor degrade themselves. And Allah surely loves those who are Sabireen." This ayah shows that even in the face of danger and adversity it is important to be patient, and faith is a companion of patience. I will strive to be patient even when faced with a hardship because impatience could cause a personal disaster and push me farther from Allah (swt), rather than closer.

"Like farmers we need to learn that we cannot sow and reap the same day." This American proverb reminds me that we can't rush certain things in life, like the growing of a farmer's crop. Patience, diligence and hope are requirements for successful farmers and for those who seek to defy adversity and gain success in this life and the next. We are a society seeking instant gratification. However, if we recall the story of the sahabiyah who suffered from epileptic fits and requested the Prophet (sas) ask Allah (swt) for a cure, we will be reminded that delayed gratification is best. The Prophet (sas) gave her two options: one, be patient and obtain paradise or two, he could pray for the cure. She chose patience. By slowing down with patience, I can gain or experience things I wouldn't if I sought out instant gratification.

Allah (swt) tells us in the Quran that He (swt) is going to test us and tells us to be patient with the tests. He also tells us how to obtain patience. Allah (swt) tells us that our patience in this world may gain us Jannah in the next. He motivates us to seek patience by telling us about the rewards of having patience. I can attain patience by setting life and akhirah goals. All goals take patience to be achieved. If I set goals I'm enthusiastic about, like becoming a published author in this life and a resident of Jannah in the next, I'll look forward to getting them done and be patient while working towards them.

"Patience is power; with time and patience the mulberry leaf becomes a silk gown," a Chinese proverb states. Like the wife in the story, patience can benefit you in many ways. For her, it brought her husband back, for me; patience can help me achieve goals for this life while becoming closer to Allah (swt).

Special Speech
Mohina Shomuratova, Springfield, Va.
5th Grade, Al-Qalam Academy

The purpose of writing this essay is so we can have more knowledge on sabr, and teach it to others. Sabr is an Arabic word for patience. Sabr is an important virtue in Islam. During times of deep trial, despair, and sadness, Muslims seek comfort and guidance in the words of Allah (swt) in the Quran. Allah (swt) reminds us that all people will be tested in life, and calls upon Muslims to bear these trials with patience and prayer Indeed, Allah (swt) reminds us that many people before us have suffered and had their faith tested so we too will be tested in this life.

Imam al-Sadiq said, "Whoever of the believers that bears patiently with a tribulation that befalls him, has the reward of a thousand martyrs." Patience is half of iman. iman is in two halves, half is patience (sabr) and half is gratitude (shukr). It is said in the Quran, Surah Baqarah, ayah 153, that Allah (swt) is with the Sabireen. Sabireen is an Arabic word for patient people. Iman is based on two pillars, yaqeen (conviction) and patience, which are referred to in Surah Sajdah, ayah 24, "And We appointed, from among them, leaders, giving guidance under our command, so long as they persevered with patience and continued to have faith in our Signs." Imam al-Sadiq said, "When a believer enters his grave, salah is on his right hand, zakat is on his left, virtue faces him, with sabr taking him under its shelter. When the two angels charged with questioning enter upon him, sabr says to salah, zakat and virtue: take care of your companion, if you fail to assist him I will take care of him myself!"

Prophet Muhammad (sas) was a role model for practicing patience. At the time, when he started preaching Islam, the non-believers tried their best to hurt Prophet Muhammad (sas) and cause him problems. Prophet Muhammad (sas) never lost his patience. He taught people to have good manners and be patient in the times of hardship. However, people today lose their patience in times of hardship. Allah tells us to be patient in the face and from the mouth. We must all look upon the Prophet (sas) and follow his path of forgiveness and patience's to gain success in every walk of life. Prophet Muhammad (sas) said, "No one can be given a blessing better and greater than patience."

When the people discovered that Prophet Ibrahim (as) destroyed their idols, they wanted to kill him by throwing him into a fire. So they set the fire and threw him into it. Prophet Ibrahim (as) did not yell or run, but he was patient and made duaa to Allah saying, "Allah Alone is enough for us, and he is the Best Disposer of affairs." It is said in the Quran, Surah Anbiya, ayah 69 that Allah (swt) said, "O fire, be coolness and safety upon Ibrahim."

Prophet Yusuf (as) was a patient man. When his brothers threw him into the well, he had to stay there for three days and three nights. He went to prison for a crime he did not commit. He stayed patient, and never lost hope in Allah (swt).

Allah (swt) has given us three types of patience, the first type of patience is when obeying Allah (swt) and finding it hard to do so. For example, waking up early for the Fajr prayers. We should be patient and show gratitude when carrying out these deeds. The second type of patience is when a trouble befalls you, for example, a loss of a property or family. We should be patient at these times. The third type of patience is when finding it hard to abstain from sins. For example, when a person listens to music and then finds out it is not allowed in Islam to listen to music, this person tries their best to stop from listening to music.

Khadija bint Khuwaylid is an example of a patient woman. She was the first wife of Prophet Muhammad (s). She was the first Muslim woman in Islam. She did not hesitate for a moment to accept his call, she was the first person to have faith in and believe in him. She supported him in his call. She was patient at all times. One day, Prophet Muhammad (sas) gave Khadija the good news that Allah said salaam to her and promised her a house in Jannah built of pearls where there would be no noise. She was the most patient and supportive woman of her time.

Work Cited
Huda. "Patience, Perseverance, and Prayer." Web. http://islam.about.com/od/prayer/a/patience.htm

Essay Panel Contest
2011

This poster was submitted by Nuha Mahboob and won 1st Place honors in Level 4.

Patience: How Do I Achieve It?

LEVEL 4: Grades 7 & 8

1st Place
Zaynab Gholston, Columbia, Md.
8th Grade, Homeschool

"Patience is bitter, but its fruit is sweet," Jean Jacques Rousseau once said. "How poor are they who have not patience! What wound did ever heal but by degrees," Shakespeare once wrote. These are quotes about patience, but more importantly is what Allah (swt) says in Surah Al-Imran, ayah 146. "Allah loves those who are the Sabireen." Having sabr assists in decision-making, lowering stress levels and increases nearness to Allah (swt). It can be achieved through slowing down, assessing situations before making decisions, by reading the Quran, and by praying.

In the Quran, Surah Al-Imran, ayah 146, Allah says, "And many a prophet fought and a along with him large bands of religious men. But they never lost heart for that which did befall them in Allah's Way, nor did they weaken nor degrade themselves. And Allah (swt) loves As-Sabireenn." How hard would it be to face a hardship and still keep your head held high with determination without degrading yourself. Without faith in Allah (swt) and belief that you were being purified, it would be very hard. This ayah means when faced with hardships, handling them with patience and perseverance will bring nearness to Allah (swt) and rewards.

"The key to everything is patience. You get the chicken by hatching the egg, not smashing it." Arnold H. Glasgow once said. "Patience is the key to contentment," a proverb goes. Persevering with patience brings Allah (swt)'s reward, and obtaining patience itself has its own benefits. Having patience reduces stress levels by preventing anger and frustration; therefore, in difficult situations becoming overwhelmed can be avoided. Reducing stress allows one's pace to slow down and think about the decision to be made. Therefore, having patience can also result in easier and better decision-making. With patience, one can take time to see the ups and downs of a decision and deduce the best option. Patience is rewarded with peace, easier decision making, lower stress levels and an overall better life experience.

Patience has many great benefits, but to get those benefits patience must first be attained. One way to do this is by slowing down; it's something our human kind rarely do. We often say "I'm late for work," "I'm going to miss the bus," or "I have this and that to do." Media and technology is constantly speeding things up. There's quicker text messaging, faster internet and downloading. Instead of going out for grocery shopping, it can be done from a computer with a few simple clicks of a mouse. Maybe somewhere in the future pre-written biology essays will be bought off the shelves and turned in due to lack of patience. Reading the Quran and praying regularly is definitely part of slowing down. By taking the time to slow down and pray or read a juz of Quran patience is exercised and increased. Still, patience is not something once obtained is owned forever, one must keep exercising patience. As Henry Wadsworth Longfellow states, "All things come round to him who will but wait." This is a perfect example of how patience is tied together with slowing down. The person who slows down and waits with patience is the person who will ultimately get what they need.

Reflecting on a situation before acting is another way to exercise patience. It's something that everyone in their daily lives can do and it's something that can change a situation entirely. Allah (swt) says in the Quran, "O you who have believed, seek help in patience and prayer; surely Allah (swt) is with the patient" (2:153). By seeking patience and praying, a decision could change for the better. Simply take a look at this proverb: "One moment of patience may ward off great disaster. One moment of impatience may ruin a whole life." Reflecting on a decision could either help a person pass a test or completely fail. Situations should be reflected on before making any decision, whether the decision is answer choice A or B, or whether a student should report a bully or not.

Allah (swt) loves those who are patient and Muslims will be rewarded for being patient during times of hardships. Patience has many benefits which include, lower stress levels and better decision making. In order to get these benefits, one must have patience, which can be achieved by slowing down, taking the time to think before action, reading Quran and making daily prayers. There are many ways to achieve and exercise patience as well as many benefits. Patience is something everyone needs in their lives. And remember, as Mac MacCleary states, "Patience is something you admire in the driver behind you, but scorn in the one ahead."

Works Cited

"Developing Life Lessons." 2009. Web. 24 Dec., 2011. http://lifelessons4u.wordpress.com/

2nd Place
Juwairiyah Fatima Brown, Herndon, Va.
8th Grade, Al-Fatih Academy

Life is a complicated journey of ups and downs. Every single individual will face difficulty in this life. Allah (swt) sends us these trials to test our souls and teach us patience, sabr. Sabr is a virtue we should all try to achieve. The question is, how do we obtain sabr? There are numerous verses in the Qur'an about sabr. Allah (swt) gives us hints in these beautiful verses on how to achieve sabr. Also, if we look closely at the Arabic word of sabr and other derivations of the word, we might be able to understand how to train ourselves to practice Thirabr.

The word sabr and its different forms are mentioned in the Qur'an over 100 times. One of the ayahs that talk about sabr is found at the end of Surah Al-'Asr. It truly depicts the characteristics we must attain before we can even possess sabr: "(I swear) by the Time, man is in a state of loss indeed, except those who believed and did righteous deeds, and exhorted each other to follow truth, and exhorted each other to observe patience" (103:1-3). In the first ayah of this beautiful surah, Allah (swt) strongly states that every single person is in loss. After He states this, the last ayah excludes those who maintain the following: belief, righteous deeds, exhorting each other to follow truth, and patience. The scholars on interpretation of Qur'an point out that Allah (swt) mentions these exclusive traits in chronological order. Meaning that, without belief you cannot move on to righteousness. In order to instruct each other on truth, we must be doing the righteousness ourselves. Then we will succeed at instructing each other to observe patience (as well as doing it ourselves). SubhanAllah, it is all laid out for us in one short surah. We need to check ourselves to make sure we believe, truly believe, and then work on doing acts of piety and good character. After this we must instruct and implement truth and finally patience.

Allah (swt) promises that He will test every single one of us in this life (2:155-157). It doesn't matter if we are poor, famous, rich, female, or male we are all going to be tested with fear, hunger, loss in wealth or goods, life, and the fruit of our hard work. Allah (swt) also gives good news to the people who patiently persevere when the promised calamities arrive. How are these people patient? Ayah 156 goes on to explain that those people are unique because when a difficulty strikes, they remind themselves of Allah (swt) by saying, "Indeed we belong to Allah (swt) and indeed to Him is our return." Let's think about this for a moment. How does this statement relate to patience? If we always remind ourselves during difficulty that everything, including us, belongs to Allah (swt), then this might help us be patient. Instead of whining, we should be humble and remember we had no right to exist in the first place.

The root word of sabr means to restrain or contain oneself. Other words in Arabic are derived from this root word. One Arabic derivation of sabr translates as a tract strewn with rough stones that is difficult to cross. I found this derivation of the root word sabara very interesting because it connects with sabr. In the long run, life is full of trying moments thatd patience. The going is tough just like travelling over a rocky, sharp path. Other derivations of sabara translate as a bitter medicine, polished stones, the ballast of a ship, etc. All these meanings relate to sabr. Medicine is good for you, but hard to take. Stones can be rough but you can polish them to purify them. The ballast of a ship keeps the boat stabilized in a storm. Sabr is all of the above. It is like medicine and helps to polish our hearts as well as keep us steady in life like a ship's ballast.

As I mentioned before, sabr is a beautiful virtue we should all strive for. The only way to face the trials of life is with a patient soul and a calm heart. Let us learn from the Ayahs in Qur'an about Sabr. Let us implement sabr so we can have a great reward. May Allah (swt) help us to be among those who have sabr. Ameen.

3rd Place
Amirah Ahmad, Greenbelt, Md.
8th Grade, Tarbiyyah Academy

Jannah is what we all want right? To earn it, we must be successful. What does that have to do with patience? Allah (swt) says about those who are patient, "Those are the guided ones." Patience leads to guidance, guidance leads to success, and success leads to Jannah. See how it connects? So to achieve Jannah, we must first achieve patience. Throughout this essay, I will explain how to achieve the different kinds of patience through the controlling of anger, persistence, and self-control.

Have you ever been in a situation where someone was bothering you on purpose?

I know that I have, and in a time like that, I would have two choices: be patient or get angry. Chances are that if I get mad and tell them to stop, they will just keep doing it, especially if it is my younger brother. If, however, I choose to be patient, they will realize they are not achieving their purpose and leave me alone. If you noticed, I used the word choose. A person has to choose to be patient; it won't come on its own. I should not choose to get angry because Abu Hurairah (ra) reported that a man said to the Prophet (saw), "Advise me." The Prophet (saw) replied, "Do not get angry." The man repeated his request several times and each time the Prophet (saw) replied, "Do not get angry" (Bukhari). This shows what great emphasis he placed on the subject of anger. Now if we do get angry, we have to control it, but how? William Shakespeare wrote, "Upon the heat and flame of thy distemper, sprinkle cool patience." That's where patience comes in again. In almost any situation, anger doesn't help, but patience always does. When we get angry, if we just think about this, we will realize that it isn't worth it, and Insha'Allah, we will get closer to achieving patience.

Let's say we are trying to do something and it just isn't working. If we just give up on the first or second try, it'll never get done, but if we keep trying persistently and with patience, it will lead us to success. Allah (swt) says in the Quran, "O you who believe, persevere in patience and constancy, complete in such struggles, strengthen each other, and fear Allah so that you may be successful" (3:200). Speaking of successful, don't you think the scientist Isaac Newton had a lot of success with his discoveries? He once said, "If I have ever made any valuable discoveries, it has been owing more to patient attention than to any other talent." To achieve patience, we must be far sighted and think of the outcome of our actions, whether in this life or in the hereafter. If we do it for reward in this life, for example, being patient studying for an exam, our reward will be getting good grades. If we do it for reward in the hereafter, Allah (swt) promises us, "Those who patiently persevere will truly receive their reward without measure" (39:10).

Patience is required in every situation. According to the novelist James Clavell, "...patience means holding back your inclination to the seven emotions; hate, adoration, joy, anxiety, anger, grief, fear." So even in times of joy, we should not go out of control laughing, celebrating and jumping up and down. In this case patience means having self-control. So, how do we achieve that kind of patience? Allah (swt) has gives us the answer when He talks about a time of victory and success, concerning the conquest of Makkah: "Then celebrate the praises of your lord, and pray for his forgiveness" (110:3). By doing this, we are humbling ourselves before Allah (swt), and that is a way of achieving patience. Another thing that helps a lot is looking at people who are less fortunate and thanking Allah (swt) for all the blessings he has bestowed on us.

In conclusion, the way to achieve patience is this:

1. Making the choice to remain patient; it doesn't come automatically.
2. Understanding the fact that being impatient never helps in any situation, but remaining patient always does.
3. Constancy and perseverance; not giving up.
4. Thinking about the outcome of your actions; what the reward or punishment might be.
5. Having self-control in all different kinds of situations and not allowing your nafs to take over.
6. Thinking about all the people around the world who have less than you, and being grateful for what you have.

Insha'Allah, if we follow these guidelines, we will be able to achieve patience and understand how essential it is to us as mentioned in the hadith narrated by Abu Hurayrah and Abu Sa'id in which the Prophet (saw) says, "How wonderful is the case of a believer. There is good for him in everything. If prosperity attends him, he expresses gratitude to Allah (swt) and that is good for him; and if adversity befalls him, he endures it patiently and that is better for him" (Muslim).

Special Essay
Zaakira Ahmed, College Park, Md.
8th Grade, Al Huda Hifzh School

Stop. Don't do it. As I contemplate confronting my classmate about a rumor she has started about me and take my revenge, my mind is telling me not to do it. Patience, my dear. Patience. The quality of delaying feelings of annoyance, misfortune, or pain when afflicted with hardship. These days, I am being forced to learn about this important virtue, as my parents keep reminding me that I am held accountable for my every action. "Patience, sabr, is one of the greatest characteristics of a Muslim," my father says. However, as I sit here thinking, how can I possibly not get upset by the fact that someone I thought was my friend, was going around spreading lies about me? Why is it wrong for me to want to face her and tell her off? Why? Because "Surely Allah (swt) loves the Sabireen."(3:146). And because Allah (swt) also says in Surah Anfal, ayah 46, "And be patient, indeed Allah (swt) is with the patient ones." Hardships, no matter in what form, are supposed to be trials for us. In fact, even times of ease are considered tests for a Muslim. The only way we can achieve peace, or be in the Islamic state, is to have sabr. The fact that one of Allah (swt)'s most beautiful attributes is As-Saboor, the Patient One, is not a coincidence. This attribute of Allah (swt) is one that delays His wrath, and brings out His mercy. We should be so grateful knowing that we can use one of Allah (swt)'s most beautiful names to get closer to Him.

When we think about someone being patient, images of tolerance, being passive, and being without feelings come to mind. However, having Sabr as a Muslim is much deeper than that. While we appear as if we're sitting around letting people take advantage of us, a believer is earning rewards from Allah (swt). He knows that panicking or getting angry and frustrated isn't going to change what Allah (swt) has already written for him. We all know some people who go about their days complaining about everything that happens to them and walk around as if their lives are extremely miserable. We know people who blow up over little things, or people who never have anything good to say. These are bad examples for a Muslim, and we shouldn't use them to steer our behavior. The only example that we should follow is that of the Prophet Muhammad (sas). Prophet Muhammad (sas) was the embodiment of patience. If he could face the hardships he went through and still come out smiling, remain gentle and kind, and not forget about his ultimate goal, who are we to complain about the small trials Allah (swt) tests us with? We have not learned about the Prophet (sas) threatening anyone or taking revenge on anyone. The Prophet Muhammad (sas) was so forgiving and even made du'a to Allah (swt) to change the hearts of the kuffar. The Prophet (sas) taught us in a hadith that, "Strange are the ways of a believer, for there is good in every affair of his, and this is not the case with anyone else except in the case of a believer; for if he has an occasion to feel delight, he thanks Allah (swt); thus there is good for him in it, and if he gets into trouble, and he endures it patiently, there is good in it for him" (Muslim). Prophet Muhammad (sas) and all the other Prophets were tested over and over again by Allah (swt) and they all came out successful.

Being patient in times of difficulty has many benefits. You are able to think more clearly in a situation. Your mind becomes sharper when you stay calm and you are also able to make better decisions. Patience breeds a positive attitude toward life as well. You find yourself always looking at the positive side of things. Patient people also tend to be more successful in all that they do because they realize that most good things take time and effort to achieve. Furthermore, the most important benefit of being patient is that Allah (swt)'s reward is doubled as stated in Surah Qasas, ayah 54, "Those will be given their reward twice for what they patiently endure."

Insha'Allah, I will exercise patience by reciting the tashahud before acting on an impulse. I will remember what is more important in life before becoming impatient and possibly hurting someone's feelings. I will also try to remind myself that, when I'm in difficult situations, becoming angry, frustrated, or feeling hopeless will not change Allah's will. To pass the test, I must have patience. So the next time my little siblings take something of importance to me and break it or lose it, I will have to hold back tears and realize that maybe Allah is protecting me from something bad. And the next time my mom tells me I can't have the latest gadget that all my friends have, I'll have to patiently accept the fact that it's probably not the right time for me to have it yet. And maybe, just maybe, when my classmate comes up to me after days of spreading rumors, and apologizes for lying and being insensitive, I will forgive her and patiently await the consequences of her negative actions- which, by the way, I never heard about. Allah loves those who are patient and my goal is to achieve that love. One of my great role models, Helen Keller, once said, "We could never learn to be brave and patient if there was only joy in the world." She couldn't have been more right.

Works Cited
Abd AlShafy, Magdy. "Prophet Muhammad: Infinite Patience." 2010. Web. http://www.quran-m.com/firas/en1/index.php?option=com_content&view=article&id=436:prophet-muhammad-infinite-patience&catid=51:prophetical&Itemid=105

Amatullah. "Six Benefits of Patience from the Qur'an " http://www.suhaibwebb.com/personaldvlpt/character/six-benefits-of-patience-from-the-quran/

Hameed, Shahul. "The Prophet's Inexhaustible Patience, A Muslim Reflects." Web. http://www.usislam.org/islamicyouth/Muhammad/prophets_inexhaustible_patience.htm

"The Virtues of Patience." Web. http://www.inter-islam.org/Lifestyle/patience.htm

Special Speech
Shad Khan, Centreville, Va.
7th Grade, Ormond Stone Middle School

A wise person once said, "All good things come to those who wait." What is this person talking about? Patience. Patience means a person's ability to control anger, emotion, and troubling situations. Here, I will explain an ayah of Quran about patience; explain why patience is beneficial to me, and how I can achieve this great virtue in life.

"There have been many prophets with whom many men of Allah fought; they did not lose heart for what they suffered in the way of Allah, nor did they become weak, nor did they yield. Allah surely loves those who are the Sabireen." (3:146). This ayah explains that there have been many people of the prophets who have fought to defend and support their cause (that is, Islam). They never became weak, gave up, or lost heart for their cause. They never lost sabr.

We see the reflection of this ayah in many different Battles of Islam. The Battle of Badr is an example, where small groups of 313 Muslims were against an enormous group of about 1,000 non-Muslims. How could a small group ever hope to win against overwhelming odds? However, because they didn't lose heart for their cause, became weak, nor give up, kept their Sabr, and by knowing that even if they got killed, they will be rewarded in Paradise, they finally won.

Patience is beneficial to me. I use this attribute in every aspect of my life because:

- Patience brings peace of mind.
- Patience also avoids unwanted worry and anxiety.
- It is necessary for success. That is where the quote, "All good things come to those who wait" came from. If we wish to achieve anything of significance, we cannot expect to achieve it overnight.
- It gives us Blessings from Allah (swt).
- Patience also grants us Guidance of Allah (swt). A patient person will be guided by Allah (swt) in this world until he meets Him on the Day of Judgment. "Not so do those who show patience and constancy, and work righteousness; for them are forgiveness (of sins) and a great reward" (11:11).

"And verily, whosoever shows patience and forgives that would truly be from the things recommended by Allah." (42:43).

There are many ways to achieve patience. One way is to have strong taqwa and believe in Al-Qadr which means that whatever happens is Allah's (swt) choice and for a reason. Another way is to relax and find out the triggers that cause you impatience. If you are faced with a trigger, actively try to avoid them, recite the Ta-awouth, wash your face with cold water, and pray two rakat Nafl Salat. If you tend to do everything at once, make yourself at a Peace of Mind. Another way, don't let your emotions get the better of you. Think the blessings and favors, the wrath and punishment of Allah (swt). So we will realize that we should not respond to our emotions by doing against His commands. We should think of the special companionship of Allah (swt), as He has told us "Allah is with those who are patient" (2:153).

Abu Sa'id Al-Khudri (ra) reported that certain people of the Ansar asked the Messenger of Allah (sas) and he gave them; then they again asked him and he gave them until all what he possessed was exhausted. Then the Prophet (sas) said, "Whatever wealth I have, I will not withhold from you. Whosoever would be chaste and modest; Allah will keep him chaste and modest and whosoever would seek self-sufficiency, Allah will make him self-sufficient; and whosoever would be patient, Allah will give him patience, and no one is granted a gift better and more comprehensive than patience"(Al-Bukhari and Muslim).

Having sabr is an excellent quality to have. With it, we are guided and blessed by Allah (swt). Patience also benefits us by bringing peace of mind and avoiding unwanted worry and anxiety. Even though it is hard to achieve, we can attain this wonderful virtue by having taqwa and believing in Allah (swt)'s decisions.

Works Cited
Pettinger, Tejvan. "Benefits of Patience." Web. http://ezinearticles.com/?Benefits-of-Patience&id=496228

"Patience and Tips on How to Develop It." Essential Life Skills. Web. http://www.essentiallifeskills.net/patience.html

Essay Panel Contest
2011

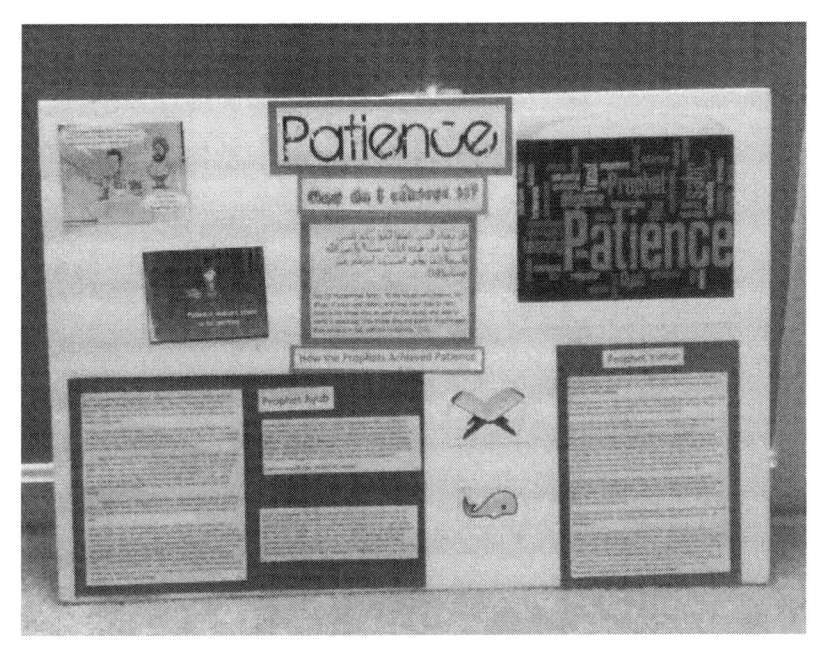

This poster was submitted by Jahid Ali and won 2nd Place honors in Level 4.

Patience and Perseverance in the Times of Trials and Tribulations

LEVEL 5: Grades 9 & 10

1st Place
Danya Chowdhury, Laurel, Md.
9th Grade, Al Huda High School

As you walk down the crowded streets in DC, you can't help but stop and stare at the many vendors. People calling "Buy one, get one free!" fills your ears as you pass. Then, a shiny looking object grabs your attention as you're about to leave. You walk towards it, excitement stirring in your head, thinking how you finally found a souvenir. You walk up to the vendor, spotting the object you saw just a few seconds ago, but notice something different. The prettiness of the jewel isn't there once you see the stand it is placed upon. It's still shining, but the display makes it seem to fade. The dirty, ripped up brown cushion below the jewel makes the whole item seem destroyed. All you can wonder about is how can a person sell such a precious item, but show it in such a valueless way? Why would someone buy something beautiful, when its appearance is unpleasant?

The same thing goes for the Muslim world. How can Islam spread its religion, when its outer appearance is awful?

The Muslim world is undergoing many problems, and the way it is being "sold" just makes it worse. Its image is being shown as dirty and filthy, just like the shiny object. These negative comments are just a few reasons to why the Muslim world is facing trials and tribulations. They must have patience and perseverance in these times where they are being known as the most corrupt, having bad quality, highest illiteracy rate, and being known as the most dangerous countries. Though they have these problems, Allah (swt) does everything for a purpose.

Corruption. This means a place that consists of people cheating, lying, and bribing others. It is said that six out of 10 countries that are corrupt are Muslims, number one being Somalia. The Muslims are seen as people who only pick leaders who pay them. They are seen to be cheating with every step they take to govern their country, their society.

Quality. At least once you might have heard people talking about moving - most of the time to somewhere beautiful. Somewhere that the people will treat you nicely and the quality of life is highly recommended. But most of the time, you won't hear about places such as Egypt, Syria, or Sudan. If you do, it won't be anything positive. If you are to search about quality life in countries, there won't be any Muslim countries among the first 35! Why? Because the Muslim world is seen with violence and social and political unrest.

Illiteracy. People who don't know how to read or write. Seven out of 10 countries that have the highest illiteracy rate are Muslims. This shows how the Muslim world doesn't know anything, and that they are falling behind in the latest technologies. They are still in a situation where they don't have enough knowledge to do anything spectacular, and so they are too poor to compete with the rest of the world.

Danger. What comes to mind when you think of this? I picture yelling, shouting, killing, people running around in a state of anarchy. The Muslims are seen as people who are always having rebellions, protests, and wars. Eight out of 10 countries that are the most dangerous are Muslim. They think that going to any of these countries would just mean trouble.

Why does this matter to us? Because seeing that our religion has so many problems makes it harder for us to "sell" Islam to those who need it; spread da'wah. There are reasons to why Allah sent these trials. Among them are: to strengthen us, prepare us for a bigger task, and our failure to fulfill our covenant. Allah (swt) says in the Quran, "Do you think that you will enter Paradise without any trials while you have known the examples of those who passed away before you?" (2:214). Everything that the Muslim world is facing is a test sent down from Allah (swt). Nothing comes free, and so in order to pass these tests, one must have patience and perseverance. The struggles that the Muslim world is facing, the problems that they are having, the difficulties that they can't seem to pass can all be taken care of with these two beautiful qualities.

What if one does not have these two qualities? The Muslim world will not only be facing struggles, but so much more. The Prophet Muhammad (sas) said in a hadith: "Rather, on that Day you will be many, but you will be like foam, like the foam on the ocean. And Allah will remove the fear of you from the hearts of your enemies and will throw wahn (weakness) into your hearts" (Abu Dawood). Why? Because of the love of the world and the hatred for death. The Muslim world is struggling, and part of this is the reason because many people are leaving their countries. They don't have the patience to stay, and so they emigrate because of their love for the wealth - this world. How does this relate to the Hadith? The Prophet Muhammad (sas) says that we will be like foam in the ocean. Picture that: the huge ocean with a light piece of foam floating on it. This is describing the status of the Ummah and how lightly it will affect the world. The Muslim world is struggling because Muslims bit by bit are leaving to fulfill their wishes, and leaving the path of their religion.

There are so many reasons to why the Muslim world is known as being corrupt, having low quality, highest illiteracy rate, and being dangerous. Allah gave us these trials and tribulations in order for us to reach Jannah and test the true believers. If the Muslims in this world have patience and perseverance, they can surmount these problems. Many Muslims are leaving their countries because of no patience so they can achieve their goals, but this doesn't mean they should stop. Instead, just like you and I, they should help their Ummah become stronger. Help them know the true meaning of patience and perseverance and the reward of it. Allah says, "Oh you who believe! Seek help with patient perseverance and prayer, for Allah is with those who patiently persevere" (2:153).

Now, let's go back to that beautiful jewel that somehow ended up on a dirty display. Similarly, the Muslim world is shown in a filthy way. Even though the jewel may not be able to be sold, it can be refurnished to an even prettier image. The Muslim world, too, can be turned into a more beautiful religion. All we have to do is have the beautiful patience and perseverance in times of trials and tribulations.

Works Cited
"The World's Most Corrupt Nations, 2011." Pearson Education Inc., 2009. Web. http://www.infoplease.com/world/statistics/most-corrupt-countries.html

"Most and Least Livable Countries: UN Human Development Index, 2006." Pearson Education Inc., 2009. Web. http://www.infoplease.com/ipa/A0778562.html

"Ten Most Dangerous Countries." Web. http://theplanetd.com/10-most-dangerous-countries/

"Lowest Literacy Rates." Pearson Education Inc., 2009. Web. http://www.infoplease.com/world/countries/lowest-literacy-rates.html

2nd Place
Zahra Zubair Nizami, Laurel, Md.
9th Grade, Al Huda High School

Imagine that you're stranded at sea. The waters are calm, as is the vast sky that reflects it. Suddenly, your boat jerks violently, and as you look up towards the once-serene sky, you see your worst nightmare: sea storms. The icy ocean waves come crashing down on the deck of your sailboat, and your crew is doing their best to keep the water out. But your boat is sinking. And as you take your last breath before succumbing to the powerful ocean, you wonder what went wrong. This is the circumstance for many American Muslims. Of course, we aren't lost at sea. But most of our hearts are. Sometimes we forget that we're American Muslims, not just Americans. We forget who we are, and in the process many leave Islam. We're losing our identity. The loss of the Islamic identity is one of the most fatal problems haunting the Muslim world today, because if we lose our identity, we lose our religion. In the instance of the boat sinking, the metaphor shows the significance of the Muslim identity, or the boat, and how when it is taken away the deen crumbles. Since the identity of a Muslim is such a prized possession, and there are so many temptations, it requires for us to reclaim it sometimes. Standing tall, remembering paradise, and spreading the word are the three steps that require extreme patience, but the ones that we should take when trying to achieve pure Muslim individuality.

The first step toward keeping ones identity as a Muslim safe is to be proud of Islam. We should be proud of who we are as American Muslim youths, and embrace Islam fully. Also, we should remember not to "go with the flow." In other words, we shouldn't just do things because they're popular, without knowing anything. However, it's not as easy as it sounds. If 85% of customers on the phone have cursed or swore, and 80 percent of customers get impatient after waiting 12 seconds, what are we supposed to do? How are we supposed to be proud of a religion that's known for terrorism? How are we supposed to cover in a society where the beauty of a woman is marketed publically? There is an Arabic proverb that says: "Fear not the path of truth for the lack of people walking on it." Thus, we should be unique and different by following not what's done but what's right. We should also follow what Allah has prescribed for us in the Quran and Sunnah. If we follow the Islamic standards that are set for us in the Quran and Sunnah, are proud of our religion and stick to it, we should be off to a good start on our long journey towards attaining perfect Muslim identity.

The second step towards attaining high Islamic uniqueness is by remembering the ultimate goal of this life: to strive for the next. When we have a focused target that we are aiming for, everything else falls into place. There is a quote by Robert O'Brien that says: "Nothing will strengthen your self-confidence more than a clear-cut, specific destination, and sticking out on the long adventure that will lead you towards it. Remember, it is a journey not of weeks and months, but years. Be patient." In reference to this quote, if our clear-cut destination is Jannah, it will strengthen our self-confidence in Islamic character. However, this could also be very testing towards one's patience since remembering something that we can't see is difficult when we're distracted by this world. When we find ourselves doing this, we should emphasize on our souls that the reward for patience is eternal bliss in Jannah. Allah (swt) says in the Quran in Surah Baqarah, ayah 155: "Be sure We shall test you with something of fear and hunger, some loss in goods or lives or the fruits (of your toil), but give glad tidings to those who patiently persevere." Likewise, we should remind ourselves of Jannah when we find ourselves under the influence of things that oppose our religion. With a fixed goal, we are almost ready to take it a step further.

The third step towards attaining perfect Muslim identity is by spreading the word. However, like everything, there's wisdom in doing this. One should give advice not only through words, but also by actions. We should watch our actions, because those who are younger could imitate the doings of ones from an older generation. Also, when people start showing signs of losing their identities, one should talk to them and advise them to stick to Allah's way. Remind them about what Allah (swt) says in Surah Al-Imran, ayah 103: "And hold fast, all of you together, to the Rope of Allâh (i.e. this Qur'ân), and be not divided among yourselves..." Remind them to be patient in keeping their identities, and remind them of them ayah where Allah says: "Allah doesn't burden a soul more than it can bear..." in Surah Baqarah, ayah 286. In addition, Ibn 'Abbas reported that the Messenger of Allah (sas), said to Ashajj 'Abdu'l-Qays, "You have two qualities which Allah loves: forbearance and steadiness" (Muslim). This shows us that Allah loves patience, so why would He not want us to have patience in safeguarding our identity?

We must think of the importance of keeping ones identity by remembering this: Life is like a non-stop boat ride in the ocean. The ocean represents the events that happen to you, while the boat is your identity as an American Muslim. It will protect you and give you shelter from the fierce winds and heavy rains only when you take care of it. Just fix your eyes on the shore, and bring as many people as you can along with you. But if you go astray and punch holes in your boat, you'll drown before you reach the shore. Never lose hope in the mercy of Allah. He'll help you fix your boat, as long as you stick to his path and try to keep your identity safe with patience. All you need to do is ask.

Works Cited
Nawawi, Riyad As-Salihin, Forbearance, Patience and Kindness. Chapter 74: 632. Web. 5 Jan. 2012.

Yiqiang Q. Z., Attahiru S. A., "Performance Analysis of a Telephone System with both Patient and Impatient Customers." Web. 2 Jan. 2012

3rd Place
Nishwath Samiya, Greenbelt, Md.
9th Grade, Eleanor Roosevelt High School

"Some are swift to anger and swift to cool down, the one characteristic making up for the other; some are slow to anger and slow to cool down, the one characteristic making up for the other; but the best of you are those who are slow to anger and swift to cool down, and the worst of you are those who are swift to anger and slow to cool down. Beware of anger, for it is a live coal on the heart of the descendant of Adam. Do you not notice the swelling of the veins of his neck and the redness of his eyes? So when anyone experiences anything of that nature he should lie down and cleave to the earth. These are two statements by the Prophet (sas) said (At-Tirmidhi). Muslims should be fully willing to suppress the anger, not exploding like a volcano. One of the biggest trials Muslims are facing right now is how to control their anger. This might not seem big or even a trial but if we knew how to control our anger and acted accordingly, we would not be facing other inevitable trials. If we do not control our anger, relationships may break, physical violence may erupt and health problems may occur; if we learn how to control our anger, we can live in peace.

Like every problem has a solution, we can learn how to manage our anger through our deen. We should control our emotions by seeking refuge with Allah from shaytan. Sulayman ibn Sard said, "I was sitting with the Prophet (sas) and two men were slandering one another. One of them was red in the face, and the veins on his neck were standing out. The Prophet (sas) said, "If he said 'I seek refuge with Allah from the shaytan' what he feels (i.e., his anger) would go away" (Bukhari). It is not permissible to show anger upon our brother or sister in Islam. Rather, we must be patient with them and strive to do good by saying "A'oodhubillahi minashaytaan irrajeem." Insha'Allah, shaytan will go away, our anger will calm down, and we will be enjoining the good and forbidding the evil. I'm sure we heard this hadith before, but did we really calm ourselves and seek refuge from shaytan? Or, did we ignore the sunnah and let our emotions run high?

Certainly, yelling, screaming, and cursing are to result in state of anger. However, the correct way to handle ourselves is to keep silent. The Messenger of Allah (sas) said: "If any of you becomes angry, let him keep silent" (Ahmad). We should be patient with the other person and be quiet. If we let loose ourselves, we may weaken unity between brotherhoods and ignore Allah's blessings. The solution is to be patient and keep our mouths closed. As always, there's hikmah behind everything.

The simple yet, hardest way to control our anger is not to become angry. Abu Hurayrah (ra) reported that a man said to the Prophet (sas), "Advise me." He (sas) said, "Do not become angry." The man repeated his request several times, and each time the Prophet (sas) told him, "Do not become angry" (Bukhari). If we control our nafs and be patient with others, we will be greatly rewarded by Rabb-ul-'Alameen. Prophet (sas) said, "Whoever controls his anger at the time when he has the means to act upon it, Allah will fill his heart with contentment on the Day of Resurrection" (al-Tabarani). SubhanAllah, if we control our anger in this dunya and persevere, Allah (swt) will make our hearts content on the Day of Judgment. Because you did not reply to the person insulting you and were patient with them, Allah will be on your side on the Last Day. On the day when people will be biting their skins in worry, pulling their hair out, not trusting one another, full of distress, worrying if they are going to Jannah or Jahannam, the Muttaqeen, the righteous, those who did not become angry, will be relieved of this stress and their hearts will be satisfied. SubhanAllah! They are on that day the most beloved to Allah because they kept themselves away from anger, struggled to control their nafs, and persevered in the way of their Rabb.

Another way to control our anger is to alternate our position and make ablution. Prophet (sas) said, "When one of you becomes angry while standing he should sit down. If the anger leaves him, well and good; otherwise he should lie down" (Tirmidhi). Abu Wa'il al-Qass said ... Atiyyah who reported the Apostle of Allah (sas) as saying, "Anger comes from the devil, the devil was created of fire, and fire is extinguished only with water; so when one of you becomes angry, he should perform ablution" (Abu-Dawood). The point is to deviate ourselves from anger –by alternating our positions- and focus on worshipping Allah –by making wudhuu'. We should persevere in the way of Allah and follow the advice of the Prophet (sas). Since we controlled our anger and are patient, Allah (swt) will surely reward us.

In any which way we control our anger, we have to be patient. Allah says, "Who say, when afflicted with calamity: 'To Allah we belong, and to Him is our return.' They are those on whom [descend] blessings from Allah, and Mercy, and they are the ones that receive guidance. Allah will reward the Saabiroon with His blessings, mercy, and guidance" (2:156-7). The Saabiroon are the ones who endured their trials without 'oof'. They are the ones who seeked refuge in Allah (swt) from shaytan, who kept silent, who tried not to be angry, and who turned to their Rabb if they did become angry. May we all be from the Sabirun and Muttaqeen and may we pass our trial of anger. Ameen ya rabb-ul-'aalameen.

Works Cited

Beekun, Rafik. "Islam and Anger Management (part 2): Strategies to Keep Anger at Bay." 2008. Web. http://theislamicworkplace.com/2008/01/10/anger-management-in-islam-part-1-strategies-to-keep-anger-at-bay/

"Anger? Islamic Way to Deal with It." Web. http://siratul-mustaqeem.blogspot.com/2006/08/anger-islamic-way-to-deal-with-it.html

Special Essay
Hager Abdul-Wahab, Springfield, Md.
10th Grade, Al-Qalam Academy

All praise and worship be due to Allah (swt), the Most Gracious, the Most Merciful. The purpose of this oral and written presentation is to enlighten the few, the ones who strive to please our merciful creator, and to present facts that many Muslims do not adhere to. In any case, the topic for this essay requires a great amount of research, inquiry, and much detailing analysis. However, as the maximum length of this exposition does not permit this, I have decided to keep this formal writing broad, yet explicit in terms of facts. The thesis for this paper analyzes one of the most problematic grievances our ummah faces as a whole. Yet as catastrophic and devastating this problem is, on the contrary, it is relatively unknown to the many. The problem -or rather barrier - that is responsible for the disunity of Muslims globally is ignorance Ignorance!

At times, this infirmity would seem overstated. However, ignorance on the part of a non-Muslim affects him and those with similar immoral character. Despite this, ignorance on the part of a Muslim affects the entire Ummah. The Prophet (sas) states the following: The believers are like a single man. If his head complains, the rest of his body will falter with fever and wakefulness (Muslim).

From this hadith, we may understand the following: that our actions contain the means of not only affecting ourselves but our entire Ummah. In this case, ignorance has been plaguing Muslims on a global level. Upon hearing this, we ask this question: What is it that Muslims are most ignorant about; politics, current events, or maybe proper cultural norms? The reason for our divisions and our counter-divisions towards Muslims of other sects is our lack of understanding of our own religion. We as Muslims are ignorant about the most basic aspects of our own religion. An example of this is our understanding of the single most important testament of our religion: the shahadah, which states: "lā ʾilāha ʾillallāh, Muḥammad rasūlu-llāh". However, the fact remains that many of Muslim brothers and sisters do not know the meaning of it. The perceptive definition of it is, "I testify that there is no god but Allah, and Muhammad is His slave and messenger." Although this interpretation may be the literal definition, the shahadah has a much deeper meaning. One of the foremost renowned scholars of our past time, Sheikh Muhammed Sulaiman Al Tamim states the following: The meaning to this quote as it goes; there is no god who truly deserves to be worshiped except Allah. It means denying all deities worshiped besides Allah.

Adjacent to this example is the reason why many Muslims are ignorant of basic principles that encompass Islam. This simple reason is that many people do not understand the Arabic language. Our religion is based on this language, which is the language of the Quran. To clarify, the primary reason for disunity among Muslims is the disability to understand the Arabic language. In this hadith, Ibrahim Al-Taimi once narrated:

> Omar (ra) went out one day and started to ask himself: How is it that nation will diverge and its prophet is one? So he sent to Ibn Abas (ra) and said, "How is it that this nation will differ and its prophet is one, and qiblah is one, and its holy book is one? So Ibn Ibas said, "O Ameer Al Mu'meneen (Caliph) we were given this Quran and we have read it, and we have understood it (including the context in which it was revealed) and then there will be people after us who read the the Quran and do understand who the verses were intended for-or its meaning so each will give their own opinion (meaning their own definition of the Quran) and if so, they become separated.

From this account, of one of the dearest of companions, we establish the necessity for understanding the Arabic language. Referring to the Jews, Allah (swt) has shown the unfathomable extent of not understanding the Quran. Evidence of this is presented in Surah Al-Baqarah. Allah (swt) reveals, "And among them are unlettered ones who do not know the Scripture except in wishful thinking, but they are only assuming" (2:78). This verse and the narration above show the necessity of learning the Arabic language. By doing so, we are much more able to understand the Quran, hence, acting upon it. The fact of the matter remains that we as Muslims are divided between one another, formulating sects of the religion that do not adhere to the teachings of our beloved prophet. Gathering upon this conclusion, the remedy for ignorance is simply knowledge.

Obtaining knowledge and acting upon it teaching requires patience. There is a reason why ignorance is bliss. One who is ignorant does not right from wrong, therefore becoming unaware of his actions and feeling no remorse or guilt. However, one who has most knowledge is most tested. He is faced with troublesome scenarios, faced with the complexity of his desires, and the evil realities of this world. Indeed, with knowledge comes great pain, and great pain requires patience. In many verses of the Quran, we are remembered by the virtues of patience and its blessings. From these verses, without remaining doubt, is a reminder for those who the hereafter. The Prophet Muhammad (sas) states:

> "…Whoever follows a path in pursuit of knowledge, Allah will make easy for him a path to Paradise. No people gather in one of houses of Allah, reciting the Book of Allah and teaching it to one another, but the angels will surround them, tranquility will descend upon them, mercy will envelop them and Allah will mention them to those who are with Him. And whoever is hindered because of his bad deeds, his lineage will be of no avail to him" (Bukhari).

In conclusion, truth of the matter may be closer to home than it seems. The late great poet Ralph Waldo Emerson states, "Adopt the pace of nature; her secret is patience."

Special Speech
Doha Nassar, Clarksville, Md.
9th Grade, River Hill High School

Patience. We experience patience daily in our lives. We see patience through our parents who have to constantly hear our whining and complaining after a long day at work. We see it through our teachers who have to repeat themselves over and over just so that we can understand what it is they are talking about; but we also see patience through the young Muslim women who are ridiculed daily for wearing their hijabs. How many stories have you heard about young girls being picked on at school because they wear a hijab? These young girls are being ridiculed, tortured and made fun of at school because they wear a hijab; yet they choose to be patient. Sadly, many girls choose to take off their hijabs instead of ignoring these insults and being patient and perseverant.

The definition of patience is to bear annoyance, pain, loss, or anger without complaining. I know of a Muslim woman, who wore her hijab for quite some time. None of her friends wore their hijabs - she was the only one. Her friends all told her that she would look better without her hijab, and so after some time she decided to take it off. In Surah Al-Imran, ayah 200, Allah (swt) says, "O you believers! Be patient in adversity, and vie in patience with one another, and be ever ready, and remain conscious with God, so that you may succeed." The irony of the situation that I have just mentioned is that this girl lives in a Muslim country where no one will ridicule you for wearing a hijab. She could have easily told her friends how much she enjoyed wearing her hijab; she could have grasped this important aspect of Islam tightly, but instead she choose to let it go. This young woman is a bright young woman, who is passionate about her religion, but she decided to give in to her peers instead of trusting Allah (swt). If a young woman surrounded by Islam can make such a mistake, than how do the girls living in the non Muslim countries react?

Girls who live in non Muslim countries like America are extremely patient. A Muslim girl is walking to class one day when another student comes up to her and asks, "Hey are you a terrorist?" After 9/11, many people have been looking at Muslims as terrorists. Sadly, some students are asked by their classmates if they are terrorists or are told to go home. In an interview with two Muslim teens, the girls discuss how they have been struggling with their hijab. One of the girls said, and I quote, " Our mom is always telling us, 'You're representing.... being extra proper because when we go out we feel like people look at our hijab before they look at the fact that we're teenagers." Not only does the struggle of the hijab affect teenagers, but it affects young elementary school children. In an article, written by the Islamic Society of Western Massachusetts, a Muslim family talks about what their children go through at school, and the harassment that they encounter. The family's daughter, a fifteen-year-old, talked about her story with hijab. She began wearing her hijab in fifth grade, and has never taken it off "despite being cursed at, stared at and pressured at school." Her mother would worry about her daughter being discriminated, but her daughter thought otherwise. "I have enough strength, I guess to, to not be afraid of who I am," she says "It's the pressure to change, people kind of hint that you don't have to wear a scarf at school, they ask if your parents make you. Combating that makes you a stronger person." As we can see from this situation, patience helps us achieve protection from Allah (swt). In Surah Al-Nahl, ayah 126, Allah (swt) says, "And if you are patient in adversity and conscious of Allah, their evil plotting cannot harm you at all: for, verily, Allah encompasses all that they do." This fifteen-year-old girl has put her trust in Allah (swt), which is keeping her protected from all the harassment that she encounters daily.

Muslims who struggle to please Allah (swt) will Insha'Allah enter paradise. "Or did you imagine that you were going to enter the garden without Allah knowing those among you who had struggled and knowing the steadfast?" (3:142). Not only are we Muslims supposed to be patient, but we are to be steadfast and perseverant. Steadfast means to stay firmly fixed in place. Perseverance means to persist and continuously pursue a goal or objective despite continuous challenges and hardships. Anas (ra) said that the Prophet (sas) said, "Allah said: If I test my slave by depriving him of his two precious ones (meaning his eyes or eyesight), and he faces that with patience, perseverance, I shall compensate him with paradise" (Bukhari). In this hadith, you can see that being patient even though you have been put in a hardship - in this case loss of sight - will help you reach the most magnificent place ever: paradise.

We struggle daily and we must remind ourselves to be patient. The more a Muslim struggles for Allah (swt)'s cause, the more Allah (swt) will reward him. It is important to obey Allah (swt), by doing what he has asked of us. As Muslims we should take pride in our religion, no matter what the cost is. Remembrance of Allah (swt) is one of the best ways to help us improve our patience. This is because whenever we do something good, we will be reminded of Allah (swt)'s blessings, which will cause us to try to spend more time doing good. The extra time spent on doing good will help us increase our patience. Being patient may be difficult for some people, and it may be a piece of cake for others, but no matter where our patience level is we should always strive to become better Muslims. So when you go home today and you find yourself about to lose your patience by getting into an argument, stop and remember: And Allah loves those who are patient in adversity.

Works Cited
Nassar, Ayman. Mountain Strong: Patience in Practice. Islamic Leadership Institute of America, 2009

Woodruff, Judy. "The Inner Journey of Young Muslims in America: NPR." NPR : National Public Radio: News & Analysis, World, US, Music & Arts: 2006. Web. Dec. 2011. http://www.npr.org/templates/story/story.php?storyId=6080584

Yahya, Harun. "The Importance of Patience in the Quran." An Invitation to The Truth. Web. Dec. 2011. http://www.harunyahya.com/patience03.php

"Young Muslim American Face Bullies of All Ages With Resilience | Islamic Society of Western Massachusetts." Islamic Society of Western Massachusetts 12 Sept. 2011. Web. Dec. 2011. http://www.masjidma.com/2011/09/12/young-muslim-american-face-bullies-of-all-ages-withresilience

"What did the Prophet (sas) say about Patience?" Zaufishan. 20 Apr. 2011. Web. Dec. 2011. http://www.zaufishan.co.uk/2011/04/what-did-prophet-say-about-patience.html

Essay Panel Contest
2011

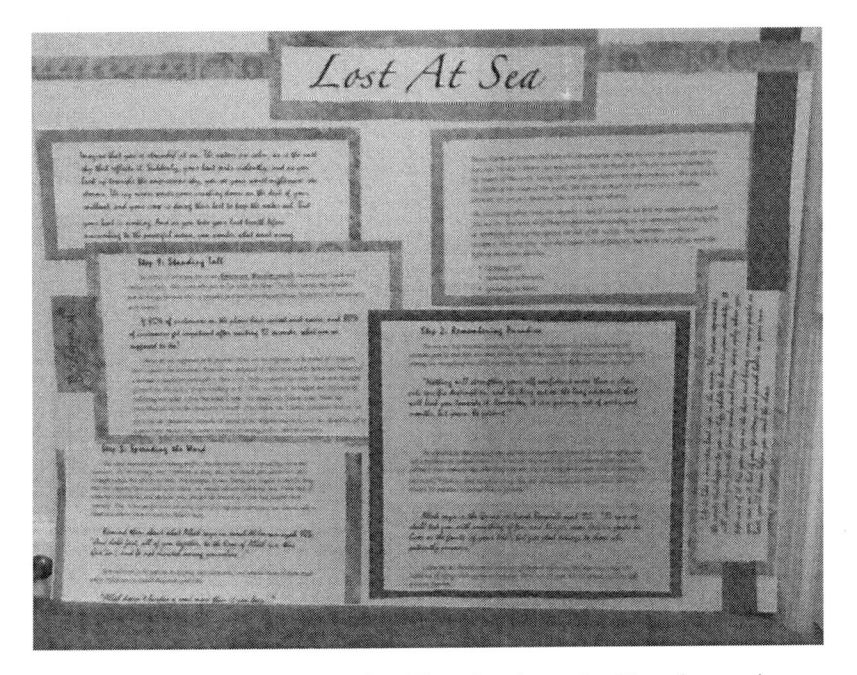

This poster was submitted by Zahra Nizami and won 1st Place honors in Level 5.

Patience and Perseverance in the Times of Trials and Tribulations

LEVEL 6: Grades 11 through College

1st Place
Sarah Arafat, Baltimore, Md.
11th Grade, Western School of Technology and Environmental Sciences

Respect, determination, honesty, responsibility, and loyalty are five qualities every human being on this planet, Muslim or not, should strive to perfect. The two that I haven't mentioned, patience and perseverance, are especially important. My personalized definition of patience is the ability to take a situation with grace and not rush an outcome. Our Prophet Muhammad (sas) said, "Patience is half of faith." Now perseverance is the way one is able to stick with a choice made until the goal is reached. In the hard times of trials and tribulations, patience and perseverance can guide one through the somewhat dark times we lightly call life's unpleasant surprises. Patience and perseverance are two important qualities that are helping Muslims in the Middle East achieve representation from their nations' leaders.

The leaders of Egypt, Syria, and Libya have either finally been kicked out or are nearing that outcome. In all three of these countries, the protesters have had to exhibit great patience as they waited for their leader to fall. Their strategy was clever. They communicated through Facebook and organized peaceful protests. The government had a hard time understanding that the people didn't want them anymore. When they finally understood, but didn't like that idea, they started harming the protesters. Yes, the government was hurting its own people. Egypt's dictator, Hosni Mubarak, fell from power on February 11, 2011 and after 18 days of protesting. Muammar Gadhafi of Libya died on October 20, 2011. The president of Syria, Bashar Al-Assad, is still in power but, if the pattern continues, the end for him is also near.

The Muslims in these countries need to pray and make du'aa to Allah (swt) for what they want. They need to be patient because success can't be achieved overnight. The famous Martin Luther King stated, "For all of us today, the battle is in our hands. The road ahead is not altogether a smooth one. There are no broad highways to lead us easily and inevitably to quick solutions. We must keep going."

The followers of Prophet Muhammad (sas) always tried to be patient in times of trials and tribulations therefore they are a perfect example of what we should strive to be. Prophet Muhammad's (sas) followers were patient and persevered for thirteen years in Makkah while being discriminated against, mistreated, and treated unequally. They also endured physical abuse resulting in them migrating to Medina when even then they were patient for eight more years because of the wars of Badr, Uhud, and Al- Khandak until their victory over the Makkans. Since they had to migrate, they left with only the belongings they could carry. Imagine how hard it is for us to leave our belongings for any span of time. Imagine if life was so bad that we had to leave our iPods, our laptops, our flat screens, our wardrobe of clothes, or our fancy cars because people were abusing us to an extent that fleeing was our only choice. This situation is similar in the three countries I mentioned - Syria, Egypt and Libya. These citizens are being abused by their governments, but they were patient and, alhamdulillah, now Allah (swt) has blessed them all with a chance to change the current political situation. They have persevered and according to Surah Al-Baqarah, ayah 153, "O you who have believed, seek help through patience and prayer. Indeed, Allah is with the patient."

The Muslims in these countries need to continue to make du'aa and pray to Allah (swt) for guidance. In Surah Ghafir, ayah 55, it states, "Patiently, then, persevere - for the Promise of Allah is true, and ask forgiveness for your faults, and celebrate the praises of your Lord in the evening and in the morning."

They need to continue communicating through the most effective system and, if that's Facebook, so be it. Organized and systematic communication with people you're working with will never lead you astray. They need to persevere through whatever difficulties come their way. The 200th ayah of Surah Al-Imran states, "O you who have believed, persevere and endure and remain stationed and fear Allah that you may be successful."

I have shown that patience and perseverance will be two important qualities that help Muslims in the Middle East achieve representation from their nations' leaders. I have supported my thesis with religious examples and quotes from inspirational speakers of our country. Patience is without a doubt a major virtue of life. We use it every day, sometimes without knowing it. For example, how could we drive on the road with all the crazy drivers without patience? We all have to wait at red lights don't we? Now perseverance is a more personal virtue. In order for perseverance to be used, you need a goal. The Arabs in the Middle East had one goal: To get their lives back on track with a new political leader that had their best interests in mind. They wanted to live in a country that was safe and one in which they could raise a family. They persevered through all the difficulties that presented themselves, and they are now starting to reap some of the rewards. Their original goal may not be fully attained until a little later, but as Francis of Assisi said, "Start by doing what is necessary; then do what is possible; and suddenly you are doing the impossible."

2nd Place
Adib Laskar, Lanham, Md.
11th Grade, Eleanor Roosevelt High School

Patience and perseverance are two very similar characteristics that everyone will hear constantly throughout their life. They both include holding steadfast through tough times and situations. For a Muslim, patience is putting total trust in Allah (swt) and as a result, Allah (swt) will ease and reduce the pain of the situation. On the other hand, perseverance focuses on strengths, abilities, and efforts that will help overcome difficulties. There are many instances and settings where Muslims try their best to exercise these two qualities. Muslims all over the world, especially in the Middle East, try their best to exercise patience when they try to fight for freedom. At the home front, Muslims try their best to fit into the modern westernized society, try to develop their Muslim communities, or give da'wah and bring other people to Islam. However, while it is advised to be patient or perseverant in the trials people go through, they are both easier said than done. Exercising patience becomes difficult when the situation slowly starts to become unbearable and intolerable. This happens frequently when many Muslim brothers and sisters come together and try to start or advance a new Muslim community. If patience is exercised through having firm trust in Allah (swt) and focusing on the future, then insha'Allah, the trial and problem will become easier to solve and overcome.

First, it is important to own an unconditional trust in Allah before we even exercise patience. To do this, we have to first believe that the trials that occur when trying to form a new Muslim community always come from Allah (swt). Allah (swt) asks in the Quran that if the believers "think they will be left alone on saying, 'We believe,' and that they will not be tested?" (29:2) and clearly states that the believers "shall certainly be tried and tested in your possessions and in your personal selves." There are many instances where common Muslims say they believe in Allah (swt) and know everything comes from Allah (swt), but they lose confidence in Him because our dua'a does not get accepted or they are not instantly gratified with the results we desire. They are told to have full trust in Him, yet they doubt Him at times when they give up or they cannot take it anymore. But to be extraordinary Muslims, there cannot be any complaints. For instance, when the Muslims in the area are not uniting to form this newly intended community, or there are not enough donations, we tend to be weak. Allah (swt) created humans "as weak, so when a sudden calamity or distress befalls on them, they become overwhelmed and often cry out, "O Allah! This is too much for me to bear!" and He "does not impose upon any of the believers a burden beyond his capacity" (7:42). Allah (swt) also intends good for His slaves. Therefore, if we take these obstacles as a test and we are patient by putting our trust in Allah, Allah will help us and insha'Allah, we will be able to produce good Muslim communities more rapidly.

Secondly, it is equally important that we find the easiest way to exercise perseverance by looking at our different abilities and trying to execute some forms of perseverance. Perseverance is not only to be patient; rather, it is to have patience and be consistent with efforts to give rise to a new Muslim community. Looking at the past, it is easy to see that the formation and the stabilization for the first and the best Muslim community of all time did not happen overnight. Rather, it took twenty years for it to fully establish itself and then start spreading its light and guidance around the world. The prophet (sas) and the early Muslims were kicked out of their own homes in Makkah and migrated out. He lost many members of his family as well as many close and dedicated Muslims. He was injured and so were many of his companions. Yet, there are numerous instances in his life where we see him not losing his trust in Allah (swt). He continuously made dua'a, asking Allah (swt) to help further the cause of Islam. It is also shown that the sahabah not only put their trust in Allah (swt), but they exhibited perseverance when they use to give to the cause of Islam and when they used to sacrifice their lives. It is reported that Omar (ra) gave half his wealth for the Islamic cause while Abu Bakr (ra) gave all of his wealth. It is reported that Uthman (ra) donated about a thousand camels before the Battle of Tabook. It shows that even though the odds were stacked against them, they were still able to remain steadfast and persevere by sacrificing what they held dear to their hearts. They never once gave up hope. This also shows that Muslims should keep their eyes on the goal ahead and continue to work towards it. There is no point in being patient or perseverant if we have no apparent goal in mind. Consider the case of Imam Ahmad ibn Hanbal, wherein he was persecuted for believing in the truth - the Quran is the word of Allah (swt), not a creation - by his own Muslim brothers. He never ceased to believe and they tortured him continuously to the point where flesh would be coming out of his body. Yet, in the jail cell, he would still educate people and would remain firm on the truth believing that one day, the masses of people will side with truth. He had a goal in mind and he stuck through it even when times were rough. Therefore, this issue should also be tackled with perseverance so that insha'Allah, a new successful community will rise from the ground and be better than first anticipated.

As a result, it is important that any group of Muslims should remain steadfast when trying to establish a new community. If he remains steadfast in Allah (swt) uses his abilities to pursue this goal and strengthen his patience, then insha'Allah, Allah (swt) will guarantee that this community will be formed. Allah (swt) will make sure his efforts will not go to waste because Allah (swt) will test his followers and will insha'Allah increase the reward and effects that will come out of the project.

3rd Place
Anika Rahman, Woodbridge, Va.
12th Grade, Osbourn Park High School

Birth and death, from the time we take our first breath, till the end of our last breath we are judged for the choices we make and watched for the prices we are willing to pay to meet our needs by Allah (sas) Life throws us many challenges and obstacles; we struggle to meet our duties, have difficulty to ignore desires and experience trouble to stay pious. In life, we face depression, sadness, and guilt. But we find healing, happiness, and hope from prayer. However this concept has been forgotten by Muslims. Today's main problem is the fact that Muslims are following the media and social groups instead of the Quran and hadith. Conformity based the American and western culture has furthered us away from Islam. This happens because we struggle to find patience and perseverance to meet Islamic duties. The media's message is like a virus that has spread throughout all Muslims ages and gender's bloodstream. Men, women and young adults are influenced to follow the wrong path and are going astray. The problem today's generation face, is the challenge to ignore the media portrayal of success and society's interpretation of happiness. Hence, to find our way back to the right path we must have these qualities to gain power to conquer our troubles and tribulation and fulfill Islamic duties.

The problem with today's Muslims is that we set the wrong price on our wants and desires. We have put a higher price on school, job, clothes, and events for the present instead of putting the right price and a stronger value on Islamic duties for the afterlife. Muslims of all ages and genders are losing touch with Islam. Wives and mothers are losing modesty. Husbands and fathers rely on pleasure from smoking and drinking. Young girls and boys are in relationships and sons and daughters have lost respect for their parents. Today's Muslims are turning into channels on television to find pleasure and entertainment instead of turning pages of the Quran to find peace and healing. We fail to read or take time to fulfill Islamic duties because it requires patience and ambition. Hence, in today's society we have convinced ourselves to forget the value of patience and perseverance as a Muslim.

We build dreams to achieve, and set goals to reach. These can only be attained through the power of patience and perseverance. Muslims are tested for these two qualities based on their actions. However, these qualities have been lost in young Muslims. We think of today instead of tomorrow. We are ignoring the fact that our present choices and mistakes will have consequences. Muslims need to remind themselves of death and near end. We must remind ourselves of our duties to fulfill as Muslims. We are wasting our precious breath on today what society calls it the life. We have taken in the words of today's society who portrays life to be one chance to do whatever you desire. This motto has adhered young Muslim hearts to pursue different goals and find pleasure elsewhere. They are having a challenge to walk away from the haram desires; we are hungry and thirsty for the wrong social groups and life. The lack of patience in today's young Muslims is causing them to starve for negative options. This is a concern because, as young Muslims, we are responsible for the future of Islamic culture.

Islam teaches us that patience and perseverance saves us from many struggles. We are constantly tested and retested based on our level of patience. We face test of challenges every day. Take the example of education: it's is hard work. Where would we stand today if our minds were not trained, if our hands were not sore from all the writing, if our eyes were not heavy from all the studying? Education challenges us in various ways. It may be defined as a test of life to evaluate our dedication, patience, perseverance and intelligence. Hence, the issue facing Muslims is not the lack of perseverance in education, Rather there is a minimal pursuit for heaven, because today we put career, beauty and desire as a priority instead of prayer, honesty and modesty, we are furthering away from reality. If we call ourselves Muslims, then we must do the very essential that separates us from the non-believers. Furthermore, many Muslims around the world are on the influence of media and peer pressure by the outside environment. However it has convinced us that beauty and happiness is achieved by pursuing the media's messages instead of Allah's message. This pursuit influenced by the media and modern cultures has made Muslims women change the way they dress, influence children to grow aggressive as a teen towards their parents, and fathers to abuse their hands from alcohol and cigarettes. The pursuit for the opposite road from haven will lead us all astray. It has been clearly stated in the Quran, "Oh you who believe! Seek help with patient perseverance and prayer, for God is with those who patiently persevere" (2:153). Surely, we can find the right path by gaining power trough patience and perseverance. According to the statistic of the United Nations (UN), Islam is now the second largest religion after Christianity. The UN statistic states that the Islam annual growth rate is around 6.4 percent compared to 1.46 percent. It indeed an amazing growth but we need to make sure that we are growing as strong, honest, pious Muslims.

In conclusion, find control of your desires, take the responsibility to make the good choices through patience, and take time to find peace and healing from the Quran. Take the courage to ignore the haram desire. Read the Quran requires patience so persevere in this duty. Take time and moments to read the messages of Allah (swt). When in troubled and good moments, take the patience to pray and ask for forgiveness. As stated in the Quran, "Oh you who believe! Persevere in patience and constancy. Vie in such perseverance, strengthen each other, and be pious, that you may prosper" (3:200).

Works Cited

"Growth of Islam and World Religions" Web. http://www.30-days.net/muslims/statistics/islam-growth/.

"Patience, Perseverance, and Prayer." Web. http://islam.about.com/od/prayer/a/patience.htm.

Special Essay
Faraz Ahsan, Lanham, Md.
11th Grade, Eleanor Roosevelt High School

They broke into his home, handcuffed him and took him away in the middle of dinner with his family. His son was thrown into a trashcan after class with his friends calling him a terrorist. His sister was fired from her job because she refused to remove her hijab. What does this man and his family have in common? They are all tragic victims of the growing epidemic of Islamophobia. Islamophobia has as many forms as a tree has leaves; it can be open hate, silent resentment, vicious harassment, and minor bullying. The list goes on. But let's step back for a moment and see just what Islamophobia is. It is the atrocious hate and irrational fear of people because they believe in Islam. This wildfire of animosity is fueled by clandestine government and media propaganda. Not only is it a problem plaguing our nation but our planet as a whole. The terrible crime facing Muslims around the world today is Islamophobia, effectively tearing up the U.S. Constitution and democracy as we know it, but this problem can be fixed through education and action.

Islamophobia is taking away the civil liberties and rights granted in the constitution. Through history, man has gained a good logical sense of what the government should and shouldn't control. Among the things government shouldn't control or change—without due process—is the constitution. Our government quickly quashes that logic with the Patriot Act. Signed into law in 2001, this abomination against the constitution directly violates the 4th Amendment, requiring probable cause and a warrant before a person or his property can be searched. The act now allows businesses, homes and personal property to be searched without either a probable cause or a warrant. Not only this, but it also violates the ECP Act, guaranteeing protection to electronic communications. This took away any privacy we thought we had in "the land of the free" as the Patriot Act allows the government to monitor all electronic communications. But worst of all is the loss of Habeas corpus. The writ of Habeas corpus is a clause in Article 1 of the U.S. Constitution; this provision allows prisoners the ability to seek relief from unlawful detention, that is, imprisonment without due process. Yet when President Bush decided to suspend the writ, taking away the protection the law grants people from abuse of the criminal justice system. Without this writ prisoners detained under false terrorism charges are left to rot in prison with no due process, a right specifically granted in the 5th and 6th Amendments of the U.S. Constitution. Furthermore, the media plays a big part in fostering Islamophobia. Bigots in the media quote the Quran out of context and lie about Islam to provide "logical" evidence to some but they also use a more subtle approach. A typical news headline might read something along the lines of "Man Bombs Hotel, 39 Killed, 100 Wounded." On the other hand a news headline to fuel Islamophobia would read "Muslim Extremist Bombs Hotel, 39 Killed, 100 Wounded." The media's only coverage of Islam and Muslims are associated with violence and terror, this subconsciously transfers to the everyday Joes watching and reading the news and leads them to believe and accept Muslim hate. Islamophobia is wrong and is a major problem in America, now how do we fix it?

Islamophobia is a disease, an epidemic, and in a hadith Prophet Muhammad (sas) said that "Allah has not inflicted a disease without prescribing a cure to it." So what is the cure for this wretched disease? Education and Action. We cannot go about correcting people when we don't know the facts ourselves. The first step in removing ignorance is to educate ourselves about Islam and about our adversaries. The Prophet (sas) said: "Seeking knowledge is mandatory for every Muslim" and based on this alone we should strive to seek knowledge. To counter Islamophobes we must know what they believe and how to counter it. Know what hadith the bigots are misquoting. Know what verses of the Quran they're taking out of context. Know the correct history of Islam, what did the Prophet (sas) do and what didn't he do. Know that only Allah (swt) can control what people have in their hearts and it's our job to deliver the message. Without this knowledge there is no hope to cure Islamophobia. Knowledge is the key to the ignition of the Ferrari. The Ferrari is a great car but without the key to turn it on it's useless. Now that we are armed with knowledge the next part of the solution is to turn it into action. While we may not change the world in one day we have to work one step at a time; systematically removing this disease from the world. We should begin by confronting those with incorrect views on Islam in our daily lives, educate them in a civilized manner and let them do with their knowledge what Allah (swt) wills. Additionally, writing letters to writers of anti-Islamic rhetoric and media companies lobbying to stop biased news coverage will – insha'Allah– reduce the amount of hate in the media. And slowly but surely Islamophobia will be equivalent to what racism is today, a heinous crime on innocent people. Moreover, we should try to work the democracy by electing Muslims in office, having them in the system will allow politicians to see the other side of the Muslim story and not just the ones they see on Channel 5.

In summary the cure for this heinous disease is a long process, requiring patience to gain the knowledge and then take the time to put it into action. Not only this but one will need the patience to deal with the many who blatantly refuse logic and the officials who continue to defy the truth and continue spreading anti-Islamic rhetoric. But Allah (swt) has blessed us with a light at the end the tunnel with his glorious ayah: "And with every hardship comes ease."

Works Cited

Abdullah, Amatullah. "Seeking Knowledge... Seeking Allah." Web. http://writerinislam.blogspot.com/2005/06/seeking-knowledgeseeking-allah.html

Abu Suad, Mohmoud. "The Role of the Muslim Doctor." Web. http://www.irfi.org/articles/articles_901_950/role_of_a_muslim_doctor.htm

"Verily After Hardship Comes Ease." Islamic World. Web. http://mudassirsworld.blogspot.com/2009/07/verily-after-hardship-comes-ease.html

Statutory Law: 18 USC §2712, 31 USC §5318A, 15 USC §1681v, 8 USC §1226A, 18 USC §1993, 18 USC §2339, 18 USC §175b, 50 USC §403-5b.

Special Speech
Shaistah Hajher, Springfield, Va.
11th Grade, Al-Qalam Academy

When the world is full of hatred, wars are bound to happen. With these disastrous events, comes the loss of loved ones, extreme poverty, the need for bloody revenge and worst of all, great confusion. Lack of Islamic knowledge leads to corrupted societies with individuals who become extremists. These extremists begin to portray Islam as a violent religion, and as always, the media is there to capture it. All over the news, we see suicide bombers, hijackers, and ransom kidnappings. All these actions are committed by Muslims. They take the peaceful religion Islam and abuse it by doing jihad. Misusing the term Jihad and doing it for personal revenge, is completely wrong. Basically, the one problem faced by the entire Ummah is the misinterpretation of Jihad and although there are many who don't understand what it is, there are solutions to educate them.

Not a day goes by in the news without the mentioning of Muslims bombing somewhere, killing hundreds. These suicide bombers believe that what they're doing is right. But all they're doing is murdering innocent people. It's mentioned in the Quran, "...And do not kill yourselves (nor kill one another). Surely, Allah is Most Merciful to you" (4:29). These bombers are fanatic people who misuse Jihad, and show others that Islam is a religion of aggression. Many Muslims and Americans are confused on what Jihad really is. Therefore, my question is "What is the real jihad?"

Jihad isn't about fighting. In fact, there's more than one type of jihad. Before looking at the types of jihad, one must understand what the word means. When you take the root word of jihad, it's "jahada," the Arabic word meaning "to strive". There are so many jihads that not all of them can be listed. But there are three main jihads before the jihad of really fighting comes. All these jihads have to do with struggling.

The first type of jihad is the struggle with one's self. This jihad contains four types of striving: striving to learn Islam, to follow what they've learned, determination and being patient while bringing others to Islam. The ones who follow this jihad, are mostly reverts. Allah mentions in the Quran,"And those who strive in our (cause) - We will certainly guide them to our Paths: For verily Allah is with those who do right" (29:69). Knowing this, the Muslims who receive the harsh criticism ignore it because Allah will give them a great reward.

The next type of jihad makes a Muslim struggle every day. This Jihad is against shaytan. Everyone has desires that must be controlled. Therefore, anything that we do that displeases Allah (swt) will please the shaytan. For instance, while taking an exam, you think of cheating. Shaytan continues you to cheat but then you remember ayah 201 in Surah Al-'Araaf, "As for those who fear Allah, when they're bothered by visitors from Satan, they remember and immediately see clearly," you quickly change your mind and ask Allah (swt) for help. But shaytan doesn't stop here. The Prophet (sas) even said that shaytan is so close to us, it's as if he runs in our bloods. Overall, ignoring shaytaan is considered jihad.

The third jihad is against leaders of oppression/innovation. When the Muslim community feels that their leader isn't ruling fairly, they have the right to go against them. They can do this by gathering peacefully. Allah (swt) mentions in the Quran, "God doesn't forbid you from showing kindness and dealing justly with those who haven't fought you about religion and haven't driven you out of your homes. God loves just dealers" (60:8). A real life example of this jihad is the Wall Street situation, the Occupy movement. These people are struggling to let the government know that what they're doing is unfair. This demonstrates that even the Americans misunderstand Jihad, because in reality, what they're doing on Wall Street is the same as jihad. These people confuse any of these jihads with holy war.

The final jihad is the last jihad anyone should practice when struggling. This jihad is holy war and it's used in specific conditions. The conditions are: the Muslim is already in a position to do jihad, the Muslim land is being attacked by the kuffar (non-believers of Islam), and their leader prepares them for war. This jihad isn't forcefully spreading Islam by fighting, but it's to protect the Muslims when being attacked. Allah (swt) says in the Quran, "Go ye forth, (whether equipped) lightly or heavily, and strive and struggle, with your goods and your persons, in the cause of Allah. That is best for you, if ye knew" (9:41). Overall, this jihad should never be the first to do, because Islam should be spread peacefully.

The problem is that Muslims and non-Muslims aren't educated about jihad. Many steps can be taken to make these people understand jihad. Firstly, we as Muslims should join in politics and news channels. By joining the government the Muslim politicians could educate the Americans about the different jihads. If we can't do this, then joining news channels can help explain what jihad is. After this, these Muslim politicians should take a stand against websites that contain false information about jihad. Finally, establishing a global wide holiday, where everyone can gather and learn about jihad. Famous speakers can give lectures as well. The holiday could be called "The Truth about Jihad Day."

All of these solutions will take time because certain people will reject these ideas. Therefore, one must have patience. Allah says in the Quran: "Verily, with every difficulty there is relief" (94:6). As Muslims we should know that Allah (swt) will reward the person who has patience. If it's hard to maintain patience, everyone should refer to the Prophet's (sas) life and the struggles he went through from a young age. Without having patience, the solutions to helping these people will fail. Therefore, with having patience, then one day, Insha'Allah, everyone will open their eyes and know the true meaning of the word jihad.

Works Cited

Al-Munajjid, Muhammed Salih. "Islam Question and Answer - Ruling on Jihad and Kinds of Jihad." Web. 18 Dec. 2011. http://www.islamqa.com/en/ref/20214/Jihad.

"Fiqh." Islam for Peace. Web. 18 Dec. 2011. http://www.islamforpeace.org/fiqh.html.

Huda. "What Is Jihad?" About.com Islam. Web. 02 Jan. 2012. http://islam.about.com/od/jihad/f/jihad.htm.

Robert. "WaPo/ABC Poll: 58% of Americans Think Islam Is a Religion of Peace™." Jihad Watch. 6 Apr. 2009. Web. 02 Jan. 2012. http://www.jihadwatch.org/2009/04/wapoabc-poll-58-of-americans-think-islam-is-a-religion-of-peace.html.

Sina. "Islam - The Peaceful Verses of the Quran Outlaw the Murder of Innocent People, Women, children."Share Book Recommendations With Your Friends, Join Book Clubs, Answer Trivia. Web. 18 Dec. 2011. http://www.goodreads.com/topic/show/188867-the-peaceful-verses-of-the-quran-outlaw-the-murder-of-innocent-people-w.

Essay Panel Contest
2011

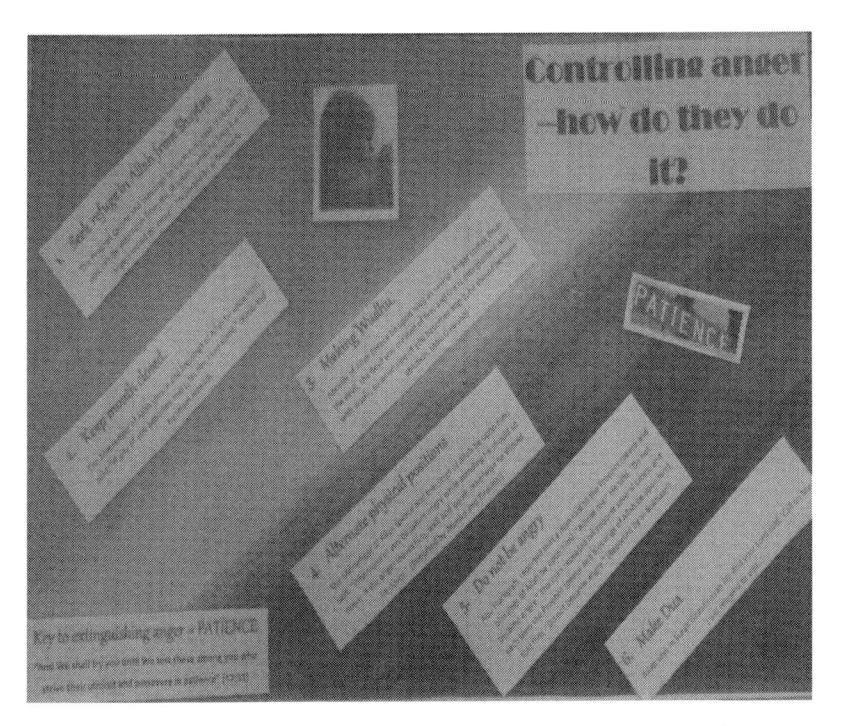

This poster was submitted by Nishwath Samiya and won 2nd Place honors in Level 5.

APPENDIX A

From the EPC Community

Participants in the Essay Panel Contest (EPC) have shared their experiences and, in several instances, made efforts to give back to the endeavor by volunteering their own time and areas of expertise. Here are some of their comments:

"The EPC has given me a lot of experience when writing essays. If not for the EPC it would probably be a whole lot harder mentally for me to stand up in front of a group of people and speak."

– Layla Gholston, competitor

"Friendly competition is always fun and the fact that through it we have been learning more about our religion ... well that's a plus."

– Zaynab Gholston, competitor

"Alhamdulillah, it was such a blessing to be part of the EPC contest, both as a judge and as a parent. Reading the essays, hearing the speeches, seeing my daughter reflect upon her knowledge was priceless. It is something every Muslim community needs and, Insha'Allah, I hope that this effort reaches communities nationwide. May Allah (swt) reward the hardworking people who take out their time and dedicate it to help the next generation of young Muslims learn about Islam in a fun and meaningful way."

– Amina Iqbal, judge

APPENDIX B

EPC Guidelines for 2011

To facilitate uniformity and streamline scoring of the essays and speeches, a set of guidelines and standards is provided to each participant prior to the competition. The following details were published for the 2011 Essay Panel Contest (EPC).

Grades 1 to 4 (Levels 1 & 2): Elementary School

Group Name	Grade Level	Max. Words	Speech Time*
LEVEL 1	1st and 2nd	250**	3 mins.
LEVEL 2	3rd and 4th	500	5 mins.

Grades 5 to 8 (Levels 3 & 4): Middle School

Group Name	Grade Level	Max. Words	Speech Time*
LEVEL 3	5th and 6th	750	7 mins.
LEVEL 4	7th and 8th	750	7 mins.

Grades 9+ (Levels 5 & 6): High School/College

Group Name	Grade Level	Max. Words	Speech Time*
LEVEL 5	9th and 10th	1000	10 mins.
LEVEL 6	11th thru College	1000	10 mins.

Essay and Speech Guidelines:
* ONLY the top contestants in the Written Essay contest of each level will participate in the Speech Contest.
** Please use a standard business letter format. Handwritten letter should not exceed three pages.

Panel Discussion Format & Guidelines:
Teams of leading Muslim youth (up to three) will be exchanging ideas with a three-member adult team to discuss the role of EPC and its impact on youth development. A five to seven minute critical analysis of the topic must be given by each panelist followed by a question and answer period with the audience. The panelist must demonstrate the importance of the topic, show diverse points of view, and generate meaningful discussions among participants and the audience. A member of the group will moderate the discussion.

Poster Contest Format & Guidelines:
Prepare and display the essay topic on a (32" x 40") self-standing poster. Poster could be a mixture of art and essay. The top three posters in each level will be rewarded.

Multi-Media Presentation Contest Format & Guidelines:
Develop an original and creative presentation of the topic using a variety of multimedia outlets, such as website or PowerPoint. Use of appropriate Islamic nashid/ Quranic recitation is encouraged. Media devices must be present during the contest. Judging is based on originality, content, appearance, and effectiveness.

Essay Submission Guidelines:
- DO NOT write your name or any personal information on the body of the text.
- Use Times New Roman, 12 point font; no image is allowed in the text. Submit simple text only.
- You must register and on a separate piece of paper provide your name, address, phone number, grade level, the school/college you are attending and the organization (Islamic Center) you are representing.
- Email submission must be in a Microsoft Word format.
- Scanned submission are permissible for Level 1 letters only. The letter should not exceed three pages and not contain your name or personal identification information.
- References must be cited using APA Format (http://owl.english.purdue.edu/owl/resource/560/01/); for Quran citation use (Sura #: Ayah #) and for Hadith use (Source, Hadith #) or APA format
- A written honor statement from the author and his/her parent/guardian must be submitted to confirm that the work was primarily done by the author (see page 77).
- EPC contest is a three-phase event: writing, speaking and publishing.
- Top contestants in the Written Essay contest of each level will participate in the Speech Contest. Therefore, preparing and rephrasing the essay for the speech is highly encouraged for all participants upon completion of their essay.
- Preregistration is required for participation in EPC 2010 contest.
- All essays submitted for this contest become the property of Mafiq Foundation, Inc. which reserves the exclusive right to use the essays for publishing, circulating, and promotional purpose.
- Final ranking for the essay competition will be determined based on totals of the Written and the Speech Contests scores. Gifts are arranged for all participants. Special awards will be given to the top three contestants in each level. Two additional Special Recognition awards in each level (one for the essay and another for the speech) will be given.

Each participant is required to submit the following Honor Statement along with his/her essay.

EPC 2011 HONOR STATEMENT

Name: _____

Grade: _____

Topic: _____

This essay was researched, organized, and written by me with no help or limited help from my parents or others.

_____   _____
Name of Participant   Date

_____   _____
Name of Parent/Guardian   Date

APPENDIX C

Glossary of Arabic/Islamic Terminology

Throughout the book, there are several salutations used to show the utmost respect to Allah (swt) as the Creator and to the prophets (as) who carried His message. For ease of reading these salutations have been abbreviated as follows.

(as) This salutation is used following the name of any of the prophets. It literally translates as: *Alaihis Salaam* – Peace be upon him; *Alaihas Salaam* – Peace be upon her; *Alaihumas Salaam* – Peace be upon them.

(ra) This salutation is used following the name of any of the Prophet Muhmammad's (sas) family or immediate companions. It literally translates as: *Radi-Allahu 'anhu* – May Allah be pleased with him; *Radi-Allahu 'anha* – May Allah be pleased with her; *Radi-Allahu 'anhum* – May Allah be pleased with them.

(sas) This salutation is used following the name of the Prophet Muhammad (sas). Although all of the prophets of Allah are highly regarded for their missions and sacrifice, the Prophet Muhammad (sas) holds a higher status as the messenger who received the words of Allah in the form of the Quran, the final and complete guidance for all of mankind. It literally translates as *SallAllahu 'alaihi wa salaam* – Peace and blessings be upon him.

(swt) This saluation is used following the name of Allah (swt). It technically translates as *Subhanahu wa ta'ala* – Glory to Him, the Highest.

In order to fully understand the concepts and principles that have been espoused by the essay competition participants, it is important to understand a number of Arabic terms that are routinely used to describe Islamic beliefs and practices.

adhan – The call to prayer made using the human voice rather than a horn or bell, etc.
AH – After Hijrah. The Hijrah, when Prophet Muhammad (sas) emigrated from Makka to Madinah, signifies the beginning of the Islamic calendar.
ajar – Reward.
akhirah – The Hereafter.
al-Fatihah – The opening chapter or first surah of the Quran.
alhamdullilah – All praise and thanks is due to Allah.
Allah – The Supreme Creator of the universe and all that exists, whom all Muslims

worship. The word Allah is derived from the Arabic word *ilah* (meaning god). The word "Allah" has no plural or feminine. In contrast, the English word "god" has a plural form (gods) and a feminine form (goddess). The word Allah should always be used in its place.

Arafat – A plain and mountain situated to the north of Makkah. Pilgrims gather here between midday and sunset on the ninth day of Dhul Hijjah to pray for Allah's forgiveness.

assalaamu alaikum – Peace be upon you. This is the greeting one should give to his/her fellow Muslims. The reply to this is *"Walaikum Salaam"* (And upon you be peace).

ayah/ayaat – A verse from the Quran. Literally meaning revelation, it can also describe a piece of evidence or proof, or a sign which leads or directs you to something important.

bismillah – In the Name of Allah.

da'wah – Inviting others to Islam through words or actions.

dhikr – Remembrance of Allah, either through thought or speech.

din/deen – One's religion, faith or way of life.

dua'a – Supplication or prayer.

dunya – Anything pertaining to this world.

Eid ul-Adha – The Feast of Sacrifice. This Islamic holiday takes place on the tenth day of the lunar month Dhul Hijjah and commemorates the Prophet Ibrahim's (as) willingness to offer his son Ismail (as) in sacrifice showing an act of obedience to Allah (swt).

Eid ul-Fitr – The Feast of Charity. This Islamic holiday marks the end of Ramadan.

fard – Obligatory act, such as the five daily prayers.

fatwa – A legal verdict or opinion given by one or more people well-versed in Islamic law, i.e., a cleric or scholar.

fitnah – Literally a test or trial.

fitrah – A person's pure state of being before it is corrupted by outside influences. This term is commonly attributed to young children and those new converts to Islam who have just made their *shahada* or declaration of faith.

ghusl – A full ablution, necessary for praying after sexual intercourse or a menstrual period, for example, or the act of washing the deceased's body prior to the funeral.

hadith – A verified description of the words or actions of the Prophet Muhammad (sas).

Hajj – The fifth pillar of Islam, Hajj is the pilgrimage to Makkah which every Muslim must take once in their lifetime but only if they are healthy and able to afford it.

halal – Lawful or permissible according to Islamic law, especially regarding food and drink.

haram – Forbidden or prohibited according to Islamic law, especially with regards to food and drink.

hijab – A veil which covers the head worn by Muslim women beyond the age of puberty in the presence of non-related adult males

hijrah – Literally it means migration and is used to describe the migration of Muslims from an enemy land to a secure place for religious causes, the first Muslims' flight from Makkah to Abyssinia (Ethiopia) and later to Madinah, and the Prophet's migration journey from Makkah to Madinah.

hijri – The Islamic lunar calendar, which began from the Hijrah, is approximately 355 days and comprised of 12 months – Muharram, Safar, Rabi Al-Awwal, Rabi Al-Thani, Jumada Al-Ula, Jumada Al-Thani, Rajab, Sha'ban, Ramadan, Shawwal, Dhul Qa'adah and Dhul Hijjah.

Iblis – The jinn who disobeyed Allah's (swt) order to prostrate to Adam (as) and was expelled from His mercy (also known as Shaytan or Satan).
imam – The leader of any congregational prayer. It is also sometimes used to refer to the head of an Islamic state or an Islamic organization.
iman – Faith, belief.
insha Allah – If Allah (swt) wills.
Islam – Derived from the word salam (peace), Islam literally means peace through submission to Allah (swt).
jahannum – Hellfire.
jannah – Paradise.
Jannatul Firdaus – The highest level in Paradise.
jazakaAllahu khairan – May Allah reward you all with good.
Jibreel – Gabriel, the angel through whom Allah (swt) conveyed his words to his prophets. He is also known as *Ar Ruh al-Qudus* (The Holy Spirit).
jihad – Literally means to struggle or strive and is often incorrectly interpreted as "holy war."
jinn – Beings created from fire, just as angels were created from light and mankind was created from dust. Known in the Western world as spirits, demons, ghosts, etc. Like mankind, Jinn have been granted free will over their actions, therefore some are inclined to do good and some inclined to evil (unlike the angels, who are compelled by Allah (swt) to do his bidding and therefore only do good).
Ka'bah – The structure in Makka to which all Muslims turn to while praying. It was originally built by Adam (as), then subsequently rebuilt by Ibrahim and Ismail (as), then finally cleansed by Prophet Muhammad (sas) and his followers after the pagans of Makkah had used it for their idol worship for hundreds of years.
kafir/kufaar – A disbeliever in Allah (swt) or one who disobeys Him or joins others in worship with Him.
khalifa – The ruler of the Muslim nation. The most honoured *khulafaa's* were the four who ruled immediately after the death of Prophet Muhammad (sas): Abu Bakr, Umar, Uthman and Ali (ra).
khutba – A sermon given at Jumu'ah (Friday) and Eid prayers.
Madinah – The holy city in present-day Saudi Arabia approximately 250 miles north of Makka where Prophet Muhammad (sas) emigrated and set up the first Islamic state.
Makka – The holy city in present-day Saudi Arabia in which the Ka'bah is situated and where millions of Muslims make Hajj every year.
masjid – Mosque; any place for worship or prayer. The three holiest *masaajids* are Al Masjid al-Haaram (The Mosque of Sanctuary, located in Makkah), Al Masjid al-Nabawi (The Prophet's Mosque, located in Madinah) and Al Masjid al-Aqsa (The Furthest Mosque, located in Jerusalem).
miraj – The "Night Journey" undertaken by Prophet Muhammad (sas), during which he traveled to Jerusalem to the site of The Dome of the Rock, ascended to heavens, met other prophets residing there, and received the command from Allah that all Muslims should pray five times a day.
Muslim – One who fully submits to the commandments of Allah.
qiblah – The direction facing towards the Ka'bah in Makkah which all Muslims face during prayer.
qiyamah – Resurrection.

Quran – The Holy Book containing all the divine revelations as a final guidance sent to mankind through Prophet Muhammad (sas).

raka/rakaat – Units of prayers consisting of a series of standing, bowing, sitting and prostrating positions.

Ramadan – The ninth month of the Hijri calendar. It was during this month that the revelation of the Quran began and the bloodless conquest of Makka occurred.

rasul – A prophet to whom Allah revealed divine texts, i.e. Musa (Moses), Dawud (David), Isa (Jesus) (as) and Muhammad (sas).

salaam – Peace.

salah/salaat – The five obligatory prayers that Muslims must perform every day. These include Fajr (at daybreak), Dhur (at midday), Asr (at late afternoon), Maghrib (at sunset) and Isha (at nightfall). Additional salaat may be performed at different times, e.g. Tahajjud, Ishraq, etc.

sawm – The obligatory fast during Ramadan, one of the pillars of Islam.

shahadah – A declaration of faith, specifically *"Ashadu al la' ilaha illahu, wa ashadu anna Muhammadan 'abduhu wa rasuluhu"* (I testify that there are no gods besides Allah and I testify that Muhammad is the servant and the Messenger of Allah).

shariah – Islamic law, derived from the Quran and Sunnah. The laws of Shariah are final and absolute and cannot be changed by human beings.

shaytan – Satan. A devil or any jinn who is inclined to commit evil.

shirk – Associating, invoking or worshipping anyone or anything besides Allah. This is the worst sin a Muslim can commit. In fact, anyone who commits this sin cannot be described as a Muslim.

siwak – A branch or root from the al-Arak tree which is traditionally used as a toothbrush. It contains natural antiseptic and is used by shaving the bark off the end, chewing lightly to soften it, then using it as you would use a toothbrush.

subhan Allah – Glory be to Allah.

sunnah – The sayings, practices and living habits of the Prophet Muhammad (sas), as recorded in the various hadith collections. Along with the Quran, the sunnah is a source of Islamic law and practice.

surah/suraat – A chapter of the Quran of which there are 114.

taqwa – The love and fear that a Muslim feels for Allah which drives him/her to avoid things that displeases Him.

tauheedd – The declaring Allah (swt) to be the only God. It has three aspects: Onesness of the Lordship of Allah (*Tauheedd ar-Rububiya*), Oneness of worship of Allah (*Tauheed al-Uluhia*), and Oneness of the name, qualities and the attributes of Allah (*Tauheed a-Asma' was-Sifaat*).

ummah – A single united Muslim community.

wa laikum assalam – And upon you be peace. This is the proper reply when someone greets you with *"Assalaamu Alaikum."*

wudu – The ritual washing with water which must be performed before every salah prayer.

zakat – A certain fixed proportion of an individual Muslim's wealth and property that is liable as zakat and paid yearly for the benefit of the poor in the Muslim community. The payment of zakat is obligatory as it is one of the five pillars of Islam. Zakat is the major economic means of establishing social and economic justice and leading the Muslim society to prosperity and security.

Zamzam – A sacred well in Makkah.